MURDERS UNSPEAKABLE

Murders Unspeakable

GEORGINA LLOYD

ROBERT HALE · LONDON

ISBN 978 0 7090 8697 0

Robert Hale Limited
Clerkenwell House
Clerkenwell Green
London EC1R 0HT

www.halebooks.com

A catalogue record for this book is available from the British Library

2   4   6   8   10   9   7   5   3   1

Printed and bound by Biddles Limited, King's Lynn

Contents

Any man's death diminishes me.
John Donne *(1571–1631)*

Introduction

The selection of murders described in this book covers almost the entire gamut of the motives inspired by human emotions. Greed, revenge and lust play the dominant roles, while feelings of rejection or persecution, real or imagined, come to a head in the paranoid reactions of men who have been driven by compulsion to act out their resentment. As always in a clutch of murder cases, sexual fantasies and perversions rear their ugly head, while killing for the sake of 'seeing what it feels like to kill', though far less frequently met with, is sometimes represented. Occasionally a killer – usually a mass-murderer – will commit suicide at the conclusion of his crime spree, unable to live with the image and burden of his guilt. This is especially a feature of some of these men who, after a shooting spree, shot themselves with their own gun.

The individual cases will be examined in detail, but I feel that a few words are appropriate here regarding what we should do with them when they are apprehended and, what to my mind is even more important, how we can help to prevent such tragedies occurring in the first place. I will deal with the question of custodial treatment first.

Prison is considered by society to be both a punishment for the crime and a deterrent to others. After all, no one would wish to spend the rest of his life locked up. Freedom is precious to all of us. So the man who kills – whether it be a wife, mistress, neighbour, employer, or a number of persons – knows, at least in his lucid moments, that if he is caught he will lose this freedom. Even the prospect of a few years in prison is enough to prevent many of us from bumping off the nagging mother-in-law or the harsh boss or the partner who beats or humiliates us at every turn. Many mass-murderers, however, are so driven by their compulsive need that they totally obliterate this aspect from their consciousness. They may or may not be psychotic, but they may be considered as mentally sick or disturbed individuals and, as such, need treatment – a combination of counselling, drugs and group therapy as appropriate. I have been reliably informed of many cases in which a prisoner in this category who was sent to jail and not a hospital for the criminally insane such as Broadmoor, has asked for medical help, realizing his need for it, and been refused. The grounds have usually been lack of resources. What an indictment of society! One would not be refused admission to hospital if one broke a leg, nor be denied treatment by one's GP if one had diabetes, asthma or some other physical disease. Why should the body be considered worthy of medical attention but not the mind? After all, the brain is part of the human body!

Where society slips up, in defining prison as a punitive and deterrent measure, is in overlooking its potential for *rehabilitation*. Surely this must be the primary aim of any sentence. As things stand, many convicts are released from prison to-day only to reoffend. They are then caught, tried and recommitted to jail, only to go through the same motions again. Conditions inside have only hardened them. Society just lumps them as 'recidivists' and gives them longer sentences in the same conditions. Now what kind of a system is that? What is the point?

Some thought should be directed towards more practical solutions than employing them on the traditional mailbag-sewing or other boring and repetitive work. This is no way to equip them for life on the outside if their eventual release is considered an option. Would they seek employment in the mailbag-making industry after their release? Of course not! Train them for a trade of their own choice under qualified instructors, and give those who desire it the opportunity of taking exam courses at various levels – 'O', 'A', GCSE, ONC and HNC, even degree courses if desired. The Open University syllabuses are uniquely suited to the needs of long-term prisoners, since the student can take as long as he needs to obtain the requisite credits.

Prisoners' work should be paid for at normal rates and, after allowing the prisoner pocket-money, the rest should be banked or invested to earn interest. Then, on release, the prisoner will have something to fall back on and tide him over while seeking employment and will thus be far less likely to be tempted to steal or defraud. Should he have to pay compensation to a victim or his or her family, the money is simply deducted weekly from his wages. It can be invested to earn interest until it amounts to the sum required, when it is paid to the recipient.

Finally, here is my solution to the much-discussed problem of sub-standard prison conditions. In reply to the government's excuse that money is short, why not let the prisoners themselves do the work? Then the cells would be refurbished for just the cost of the materials. Men who have improved the living quarters that must be their 'home' for the next ten years or more, will be much more likely to keep the cells in good condition. Humane living conditions will go far in the rehabilitation process.

I turn now to the most important issue – to prevent crime being committed in the first place. It has been proved that in many cases the mental condition giving rise to the eventual breaking-point has developed gradually, it having been apparent that 'something was wrong' even in childhood, with the onset of puberty, or in early adulthood. Several noted doctors and psychiatrists have been able to show from their studies that many of these men have a number of common factors in their earlier personality presentations. Like most diseases, the earlier a disease of the mind can be diagnosed, the better chance there is of arresting it before it becomes too firmly-entrenched to be cured. I would emphasize that this does not invariably apply in every case, but it certainly does in many, with documented cures to prove it.

It behoves us, therefore, to keep a lookout for any of these warning signs in our family members, friends and acquaintances and workmates and, should such symptoms present themselves, to try to steer the person concerned towards counselling and treatment. In this way we may perhaps be instrumental in preventing such a tragedy as those I have documented in this book.

I now give a brief résumé of symptoms, taken from the casebooks of a number of distinguished doctors, psychologists and psychiatrists in the UK, Europe and the USA. I might add, at this point, that the popular concept that a mass-murderer is a hulking brute of low intelligence is a myth. Nothing could be farther from the truth. A very few may fit this description, but by far the majority are of average height and build, average or even superior intelligence, good-looking, well-groomed – in fact, your average chap next door. As with most things, external appearances do not always indicate what lies beneath the veneer. The following guidelines may apply in childhood, adolescence or adulthood, as I have mentioned. Some or all of the presenting indications may occur simultaneously, or there may be only one or two such symptoms.

1. A potential psychopath or psychotic in the incipient stages, may be withdrawn and introspective, a loner, shunning company. Often he may have no close friends. His pursuits may be solitary, such as reading or listening to music, to the exclusion of such shared pursuits, such as playing football or other extrovert activities. He may evince an inordinate compulsion to visit the cinema alone to watch horror films, war films and other violent movies, often sitting through the very next showing and revisiting the cinema to see the same film again on consecutive days. He may consort with persons at whose homes he can watch horror videos. He may appear studious, shy and reserved, even intellectual.

2. He may be well-mannered, mild-natured, timid, quiet and retiring to an unnatural degree, never showing vexation or annoyance even when provoked. He will never fight, even if insulted, but will walk away rather than risk any physical confrontation. His schoolmates, on this account, will often taunt him and call him a sissy or a coward. He will often become embarrassed, even in ordinary social situations, and blush readily. It is hard to believe that a boy or youth of this type can later commit

the most brutal and sadistic crimes.

3. On the other hand, he may be the exact opposite, showing outbursts of temper and reacting violently if he cannot get his own way. He can be hyperactive as a child.

4. He may have obsessional traits and compulsions; some of these may be noted later at the scene of his crimes, should he commit them, such as placing a victim's shoes neatly side by side and folding their clothes. He may be meticulously clean and tidy, washing several times a day, cleaning his room all the time, and so on.

5. Not uncommonly he neither drinks nor smokes. Sometimes he has experimented with drugs, even if he does not become addicted. He is often prudish, avoiding situations such as communal showers in which he could be seen naked, and becoming embarrassed at seeing others naked. He avoids profanity, and condemns impropriety in others. He often shows embarrassment and distaste when workmates indulge in sexual conversation and 'blue' jokes.

6. Sometimes he has an obsession for Hitler and Nazism, in war beyond a normal interest, or satanism and the occult. He may amass a library of books on such subjects. He is usually fairly obviously seen to be living in a dream world peopled by violent images, and may make doodles or drawings depicting scenes of violence such as hanging. He may have an obsession for guns or knives, and make a collection of such objects.

7. He may display open hatred of one or both parents or, on the other hand, an inordinate display of love and affection for them beyond the normal range. Often he is single and still lives with one or both parents well into adulthood.

8. Sometimes he will be a religious fanatic, quoting the Bible frequently to all and sundry, even at inappropriate moments. Sometimes he will say he hears voices from God – in some cases telling him to kill.

9. The work record of such men may be poor and erratic, and their occupations are very wide-ranging. A surprising number choose to work as a butcher or in a

slaughterhouse. Such men may have been cruel to animals when they were children.

10. A man who locks himself in his room for hours, or keeps a secret 'den' such as a garden shed where no one else is allowed to enter, saying he is using it for experiments, is highly suspect.

Any one of these symptoms might or might not have any sinister significance of itself, but a combination of several such symptoms should give rise to grave concern. This is particularly relevant when a syndrome – a particular group of symptoms – has gradually developed over a period of time. This is much more likely to happen than a sudden change overnight.

Vigilance, arising out of a caring concern for our fellow men and women, may be the means of averting tragedy. An incipient mentally sick person can be diplomatically steered towards counselling, and in the case of a person obviously severely disturbed, abnormal in his social attitudes and behaviour and unable to form or maintain normal relationships, or to keep a job for more than a few weeks, the family doctor should be consulted with a view to arranging for psychiatric evaluation and treatment without delay.

Georgina Lloyd
November 1991

1

The Green River Murders

Unsolved (1982)

When police fished the nude, strangled body of a young woman out of the Green River near Seattle, Washington State, they had no inkling that this was only the first of twenty-six victims and that two years later a forty-five-man task force of investigators, drawn from city, county, state and federal police forces, would still be working on the case and yet be no further forward in the apprehension of the killer. He has eluded them to this day.

In the murder headquarters at Burien, near the Seattle-Tacoma Airport, the walls are plastered with maps, diagrams and photographs and the files are bulging with more than 60,000 pages of information. The serial slayings were dubbed 'The Green River Murders' by the news media, because all the bodies have been found either in the river or very close to it. Fifteen more young women have been officially reported missing in the area and are thought to have fallen victim to the same killer. Their bodies may yet turn up in a riverside grave.

The Green River flows close to the airport, and facing this busy international terminal is a waterfront area of the city stretching for about six blocks, known locally as the 'meat market' because of the number of hookers to be found offering their services against the noisy background of garish neon lighting, drive-in motels and bars, fast-food joints, massage parlours and strip shows. Although all the victims of the Green River Killer were abducted from this area, not all these young women were prostitutes, but nine of them had a police record for prostitution.

The victims have been white, black and Oriental, and have ranged in age from 16 to 36. From this it would seem that the Green River killer is not particularly selective, but his *modus operandi* has invariably been the same: the victims were all lured into a car and later dumped, strangled and naked. None of their clothing or other personal belongings have ever been found. Detectives are still wondering what the killer has done with all the shoes, handbags, clothes, jewellery and so forth.

The Green River killer is unique among serial murderers, who usually keep on the move, seldom staying in one area for long. The usual pattern is to strike and then move on, often before the crime comes to light; this is what makes it so difficult to apprehend them early enough to prevent them from committing yet further murders in another area. The Green River killer, however, was the exception that proves the rule. All twenty-six of his victims were picked up in the six-block strip known as the 'meat market', and the fifteen missing girls who have so far not been accounted for are also known to have frequented that area.

Not only did this untypical serial killer find all his victims in one restricted area, but he also discarded their bodies in the same vicinity, in close proximity to the streets where he abducted them. Most of the bodies were found in the river, others being left in wooded areas between the river and the airport. Most of the bodies found in the river were discovered within a short time after the girls had been killed, but others, hidden under thick brambles and underbrush, were frequently not discovered until as much as a year later, when the advanced state of decomposition made the task of identifying the remains much more difficult. In some cases identification was possible only by matching teeth with dental records. And in the King County morgue, seven skeletons are those of seven young women who have never been identified.

Detective Major Richard Kraske, heading the investigation, feels strongly that sooner or later someone will stumble across yet another lonely grave. 'There could be more,' he says. 'We know only of those who have been reported missing, but many more may be missing but unreported. Girls come and go from the area; many are runaways from other parts of the country. Many will have changed their names.'

The first body, found in the Green River on 15 July 1982, had become snagged in the piles supporting a bridge which crosses the river from the suburb of Kent to the airport. A search of the riverbank failed to produce any of her clothing. The body was heavily tattooed on the arms, breasts and thighs. The police knew that many hookers liked to have themselves tattooed, so they turned to their files on girls who had been picked up for soliciting. She was soon identified as Wendy Lee Coffield, a 16-year-old black girl who had absconded from a juvenile detention home. She had been working the strip for only two months, and was not known to have a pimp. It was unclear why anyone would have wanted to strangle her; rape was unlikely, since she was a hooker, and robbery could be ruled out. Her body had been in the water for only about two days, the autopsy confirmed.

When detectives made inquiries along the strip, they learned that Wendy was what was known as a 'car hop', who plied her trade in the backs of cars. More experienced prostitutes shun this procedure which is fraught with risk from attacks by weirdos. They prefer to keep a room in some seedy hotel among the bright lights, where at least they have a sporting chance of rescue if they are heard screaming for help.

Wendy Lee Coffield's murder did not create much of a sensation in the news media. A few lines in the local papers stated briefly that a girl had been strangled and was thought to have been a prostitute. Only when another girl's nude, strangled body was fished out of the Green River two days later did the reporters give it any attention. Was there someone around with a grudge against hookers and chose this way of dealing with it? For the second victim, too, was a prostitute.

She was Deborah Lynn Bonner, an experienced 23-year-old from Tacoma. A high-school drop-out, she had taken up with a 30-year-old pimp who had – unlike most – treated her well, even to the extent of taking her on a trip to Colorado. When questioned by detectives, he was pretty shaken. He told them that on the night Deborah disappeared she had gone alone to the 'meat market'. He had no idea of anyone who could possibly want to kill her, adding that she was too streetwise to get involved with a weirdo.

The Green River murders – albeit only two – now hit the headlines, and two days later they appeared on the TV networks too when a further couple of bodies were fished from the water. Both were black teenagers, and both remained unidentified. It was not known whether they had been trying their hand at 'hooking'.

The spot at which these latest two victims' bodies had been put into the river was an isolated, narrow gravel path running along the river-bank. No one could have seen the killer dump the bodies at this remote spot.

The 'meat market' trade practically ground to a standstill overnight. Only a few of the more intrepid and experienced hookers walked the strip. The customers, too, kept a low profile; every few moments a vice cop would stop their cars and ask them questions. Social workers were out in force advising the girls not to get into customers' cars, unless they knew them. Business was so bad that many of the pimps and their girls headed out of the state to greener pastures elsewhere. The few girls who stayed on the strip carried handguns; the gun-shy settled for a can of mace in their handbags, or a knife strapped to a thigh.

Several weeks passed, and the last two victims lay still unidentified in the morgue. Then a police artist had the notion of making sketches of their faces, which were published in all the local newspapers that circulated in the area. The sketches were accompanied by an appeal for anyone who recognized the girls to get in touch with the police.

This effort paid off immediately. Relatives at once recognized 17-year-old Cynthia Jean Hinds, who had been missing for almost a month, but no one had thought to notify the police. She did not have a record in police files, but several persons who had known her said that she had been 'hooking' since she was 12 years old – and thought that she and her 28-year-old pimp had left the state.

The second victim was identified as Opal Charmaine Mills. Only sixteen, she had been active in the church of her home town and participated in Sunday-school. She had a good record as a student in junior high and had been looking forward to graduating to college. People who knew her were surprised to know that she could have been associated with the other victims from the strip. She had no police record.

A few days later the body of another victim was found in a field bordering the airport. The area was thickly overgrown with brush and brambles, with a few narrow paths cut through to allow access for horse-riders, joggers, ramblers and blackberry-pickers. The area was also used by some of the car-hop hookers. The corpse was that of a petite blue-eyed teenage blonde. There was no identification. The pathologist who conducted the autopsy determined that the body had lain in the open for at least four weeks, and decomposition was so far advanced that it was quite impossible for a police artist to make a sketch reconstructing how she would have looked in life. The best they could do was to issue a description to the media, based on height, weight, hair and eye colour, and so on.

Within a few days of this description being published, a man came voluntarily to police headquarters and said that he thought the girl might have been his live-in girlfriend. He said her name was Giselle LaVerne, and that although she had carried identification giving her age as 21, she was actually only seventeen. He said he had met her in California, her home state, where she had been a prostitute. She wanted to leave home so that her parents would not find out what she was doing, so he brought her to Seattle. He said that she worked the strip alone and he did not act as her pimp.

The man said that her family had wanted her to go to college and that she had an IQ of 145, which is well above average. She had told her family that she preferred to leave home and get a job, although she did not specify what kind of job she had in mind. The man went on to say that he had tried to get her to give up prostitution, but she had told him that she liked the business, that it was profitable and she could work what hours she liked. Her ultimate aim had been eventually to start her own call-girl service and that some of the other hookers she had met on the strip would have been interested in joining her establishment if they could escape the attentions of their frequently brutal pimps.

A check with dental records in California confirmed the identification. Detectives refrained from telling her relatives about her chosen profession, out of consideration for their feelings, but, like the family of Opal Charmaine Mills, they could not understand why Giselle should have been associated with the victims from the strip.

Major Kraske was stymied. He frankly admitted that he had no viable leads to a suspect. The forty-five-man task force was working round the clock. They went over all the information already in the files and checked out even the slightest clue which could conceivably produce a lead, but without result. The detectives' greatest problem, Kraske said, was that everyone on the strip was close-mouthed. 'Everybody out there is scared stiff,' he was reported as saying. 'They don't know who the guy is who is killing these broads. Everybody is eyeing everybody else with suspicion.'

Hardly had Major Kraske given his statement to the media when a youth jogging in a wooded area near Star Lake, about half-way between the Green River and the airport, came upon the naked bodies of three girls, not buried in shallow graves but laid on the ground and covered with piles of brushwood, through which the feet of one of the corpses was protruding, attracting the youth's attention. The three were quickly identified as Teresa Irene Milligan, aged 16, Mary Bridget Meehan, who was twenty, and 17-year-old Shauna Lee Summers. All had been habitués of the so-called Meat Market.

Detectives picked up a lead on the second victim, Deborah Bonner, when they were investigating the possibility of a link between the earlier cases and the latest three victims. A Tacoma bartender told them that Deborah had been one of his regular customers. He said that one day shortly before she disappeared she was in his bar trying to drown her troubles in the bottom of a glass. He could see that she had problems and, since he knew her, he invited her to unburden herself to him as a friend. 'A trouble shared is a trouble halved,' he had told her.

She told him that her pimp owed money to a drug pusher for cocaine and that the pusher had threatened to beat her up unless he (the pimp) came up with the money. Deborah knew this pusher and was afraid for her life. The bartender did not know the identity of the pusher, but he did know the pimp. When detectives located him, he confirmed the barman's story. He told them that he had not reported the incident because the pusher was still operating and was, as he put it, 'a real mean guy and not one to be trifled with'.

When the detectives reported back to headquarters, one of the other investigators voiced the feelings of many of his colleagues who, it turned out, knew this man. 'A rattlesnake in human form,' said one. He had shot a man dead in a confrontation over money for drugs, and had gone to trial. The prosecutor had asked for murder one, but the jury had considered that the killing had not been premeditated and had voted for manslaughter. The man had been sentenced to only five years. Owing to his truculent disposition, he had not earned a single day's remission for good behaviour and had served every day of his term. There was even a note in the prison files that the guards had all said they would be relieved to see him set free before he killed someone in prison.

He had been out for only a short time when he kidnapped a man and a woman, who he claimed owed him money for drugs. When he eventually let them go, they went to the police, but after they received death threats, they hurriedly left town.

The Burien-based task force detectives were less intimidated than the couple who had fallen foul of the pusher. They located him and brought him in for questioning. When they searched him they found a steel knitting needle ground to a point taped to his leg. This is a well-known weapon used by convicts in prison and out. It is lethal when slipped between the ribs. A charge of carrying a concealed weapon was filed against him, but all their questioning, a search of his abode and a lie-detector test failed to link him with the Green River murders. 'I don't pound on people unless it's for profit,' he told police. 'Why should I go round snuffing hookers just for fun? It's just not on, man.'

The investigators were inclined to agree. All the Green River killer's victims had been strangled, and strangling was just not the pusher's style. They crossed him off their suspect list and handed him over to the prosecutor for the charge of carrying a concealed weapon. It was now back to square one once again.

Not long after this a female skeleton was found in a wooded area west of the airport. It had obviously been lying where it was found for some considerable time; perhaps it was one of the earliest of all the Green River killer's victims. Forensic examination proved it to be the skeleton of a girl in her late teens or early twenties, but it remained unidentified – yet another 'Jane Doe' in the morgue.

With this discovery of yet another victim of the Green River killer, the task force based at Burien was redeployed under a new command. The force was now spearheaded by Captain Frank Adamson, who had been with King County police for seventeen years and had an impressive record as a veteran criminal investigator. Second in command under his leadership was Robert Keppel, from the state Attorney-General's office. Keppel had worked on the Atlanta, Georgia, child-murder case and was no stranger to serial murder.

The first task of the newly re-formed force under Adamson's command was to go over the overgrown waste ground between the Green River and the airport with a fine tooth comb. This turned up a number of skeletal remains as well as disarticulated human bones, some of which had been scattered by animals. Forensic experts decided that many of the remains had been lying where they were found for anything up to two years. It seemed that Wendy Coffield may not, after all, have been the first victim, only the first one that had been identified.

By now the files at police headquarters were literally bursting at the seams, and Adamson requested, and obtained, funds for the installation of a computer to render more manageable the mammoth task of compiling and cross-referencing this mountain of information. The computer was programmed to compare points of similarity that might give rise to a lead, or leads, based on common denominators in the murders.

Captain Adamson has released the names of a further nine known victims, ranging from 15-year-old Colleen Brockman, Sandra Kay Gabbert, aged seventeen, and Kim Pizer, eighteen, to 26-year-old Deborah May Abernethy. In addition to these identified victims, seven more young women, or their skeletonized remains, lie unrecognized and unclaimed in the King County morgue. Twenty-six is the total to date, and as yet their killer has never been apprehended.

The most recent lead has come from a young woman who reported that while she was working the strip with a friend, a young white male with shoulder-length hair took the friend for a ride in his pick-up truck. He returned several hours later alone. When the young woman asked him where her friend was, he told her that he had dropped her off on the other side of town where she wanted to visit her sister. The young woman thought this rather odd, as her friend had made no mention of such an intention. The man then asked her to go with him in his vehicle, but she refused. She told police that she had refrained from reporting the incident because she was afraid that, since the man knew her, he could find her and kill her. She gave the investigators a good description of the man and his vehicle, and while the task force has not named this man as a suspect, they have distributed sketches and have appealed for him to come forward, as they would be very interested in talking to him.

It has now been more than a year since the last woman disappeared from the 'Meat Market' strip. Investigators have several theories to account for the sudden cessation of the murders in this particular area. One is that he may have left the state, in which case it is more than feasible that he is operating elsewhere, since killers of this type seldom cease their nefarious machinations of their own accord.

Another theory is that he may be in jail for some other unrelated offence such as burglary or drug-related crimes. Another possible theory is that he has become chronically ill, or has died.

Captain Adamson is, however, confident that one day the Green River killer will be brought to book. With the help of the new computer, assistance from the FBI, and his own hand-picked forty-five man team, he feels certain in his own mind that this deranged man cannot evade them for very long. 'From what we know about serial killers,' Adamson told reporters, 'if he's still on the loose somewhere out there, he will continue his killings until he is apprehended.'

2

The Railway Sniper

Rudy Bladel (1979)

The signalman was puzzled. Why was the stationary train not responding to his green signal? There was no reason why the night freight train should not proceed through the Indiana Harbor Belt railway yard; there was no blockage on the line, and no other trains were due from the opposite direction. John Selby, the signalman, took a lamp and flashed it intermittently towards the engine. He also leaned out of the window of his control cabin as far as he could and blew a piercing blast on his whistle. It would be Roy Bottorff driving that engine, Selby knew. Even if Roy had been taken ill at the controls, there was still Paul Overstreet, his fireman, who could take over in an emergency. There was no response, however, and the train stood ominously silent.

Selby decided to investigate. Lighting the way with his lamp, he climbed down the iron steps from the signal-box to the ground beside the track. He walked towards the big locomotive, and as he came level with it he saw that Roy Bottorff's head was hanging out of the window as though he were intent on examining the wheel below.

'Hi!' Selby called out. 'You got a problem?' There was no reply. The driver did not move, or even look up. Selby set the lamp on the ground and hoisted himself up into the cab of the engine. The inside light was on. It was then that he saw the fireman, Paul Overstreet, in his seat at the controls. He appeared to be leaning back, his arms hanging limply at his sides. Roy's body was grotesquely twisted, as though he had tried to lean sideways to look out of the window. There was blood on his shirt. Paul, too, had blood on his head and neck. The two men looked very obviously dead.

Selby clambered down from the cab of the engine and made all haste to his signal-box, leaving the lamp standing on the ground at the side of the track to mark the spot. There was a cumbersome, old-fashioned black telephone in his control cabin, but it worked. He called his supervisor, Frank Ashley, to report what he had found, then called police, who were quickly at the scene.

There was nothing that could be done for the driver and his mate. Two .22 calibre shells had been fired into each of them. Roy had been shot through the heart and lungs; Paul through the head and neck. The shots had killed them instantly.

Detectives cordoned off the area and used Selby's lamp to begin an inch-by-inch search of the track. Spent shell casings were found both inside the cab of the engine and on the track beside the train. No other clues were forthcoming, and the police now turned their attention to the problem of attempting to ascertain what motive the killer could have had for shooting these two well-liked men, neither of whom had ever been in any trouble with the law, nor did they associate with any dubious characters. No shots had been heard by Selby or anyone else, so it was presumed that a silencer had been used.

A review of the circumstances of the killings showed that the assassin had timed his attack with precision, choosing an occasion when the train was stationary, which seemed to point to the killer having some knowledge of the movements of railway traffic. He had also been a good marksman. It was difficult to pinpoint the precise location from which the shots had been fired, since there were several places which would have provided cover nearby. The train had been an interstate freight hauler, so the police at the nearest town of Hammond called in the FBI.

The night of 3 August 1963 was hot and humid, and it

was with relief that John Selby had been allowed to go home after questioning by detectives. A relief signalman was quickly rustled up by Frank Ashley, the railway yard supervisor at Indiana Harbor Belt Depot, and the bodies of the victims removed to the morgue, the engine uncoupled and shunted into sidings, and placed under police guard. The rolling stock with its freight was assigned to another locomotive and allowed to proceed to its destination. Meanwhile the gunman had disappeared without trace, no motive had been established, and no leads surfaced. Finally the police were forced to admit defeat, and although the file was not closed it was allowed to slip into limbo. The 'unsolved' stamp was never one that police liked to use on any of their cases, but this time they had no choice.

*   *   *

Five years later, on 6 August 1968, in the railway yard at Elkhart, Indiana, engine driver John Marshall was just about to board his locomotive when he suddenly felt a sharp, searing pain in his groin. A moment later oblivion swept over him as two bullets entered his head. He slumped to the ground before he could climb into the cab. No shots were heard, so it was some time before other railway workers found his body. The shots to the head had killed him instantly.

Police determined that he had been shot at fairly close range. Questioning of various railway employees elicited the information that a stockily built man with an odd loping gait had been seen leaving the yard shortly after the estimated time of the murder. The man had a soft hat pulled down over his face, so that his features were hidden.

Police were unable to come up with a single clue except this rather tenuous lead; after all, stockily built men who wore slouch hats were legion. Anyone could enter and leave the railway yards on legitimate business. The detectives were not yet ready to talk in terms of a pattern, but they did of course recall the previous shootings at Indiana Harbor Belt Depot, which had taken place five years earlier almost to the day – those on 3 August, this one on 6 August. All the victims had been killed with .22 bullets. Was there a connection?

As in the previous case, the police were bogged down by the complete lack of evidence into inactivity, and once again the investigation was rubber-stamped 'Unsolved'. Railwaymen who remembered the double shooting of 1963 privately thought that there *was* a connection, whatever the police might say. Some even voiced the opinion that a man with a grudge against the railways had committed both the crimes. But they dismissed the idea of a member of the public with a grievance because of repeated inconvenience through the failure of trains to arrive on time. Such a person would not seek out the men who drove freight locomotives as targets.

* * *

The shootings had been all but forgotten when, eight years later, train driver James McCrory was sitting in the cab of his engine in the Elkhart freight yards on 5 April 1976, waiting for the signal to move off. Before he could do so, a shotgun bullet hit him in the head, killing him instantly. Again there were no clues and no leads, and again the killing remained unsolved. This time even the police were considering the killings to be connected. The newspaper headlines dubbed the killer the 'Railway Sniper', and railwaymen, particularly those working in the goods yards, were becoming apprehensive, jumping at shadows and looking over their shoulders. All their vigilance, however, availed them nothing.

In Jackson, Michigan, on New Year's Eve of 1978, conductor William Gulak and guard Robert Blake were waiting in the station office to take out the train to Detroit, which had not yet arrived. The time was seven o'clock; in just five hours they would be seeing the New Year in aboard their locomotive. Instead, a man carrying a twelve-bore shotgun silently entered the office, pointed the gun at the two men as they sat talking, and shot them both dead at point-blank range. He then left as silently as he had entered, walking quickly out of the office on to the platform. A fireman, Charles Burton, just happened to be in the wrong place at the wrong time, coming along the platform towards the office to record his time in the log as he began his shift and looked up to see who was coming from the office. The mystery marksman eliminated him as a potential witness with one blast.

Hearing shots, the station-master and a ticket-booth salesman rushed on to the platform, but the killer was nowhere to be seen. They tended the stricken fireman and called an ambulance, which arrived very quickly and rushed him to the University Hospital in Ann Arbor. Charles Burton died shortly after his arrival in casualty.

Police found a witness – though not a railway employee – who had been on the point of entering the station, who said that he had seen a 'hulking figure' of a man, wearing a knee-length greatcoat and a slouch hat, walking quickly away. Since it was dark, the witness had been unable to see his face. He said that the man appeared to be carrying an object of some kind hidden inside his coat. Apart from this sighting, the police had nothing else to go on. There was now no doubt in the mind of any of them that there was quite definitely a connection. Seven railwaymen had been shot dead over a period of fifteen and a half years, all within one part of the Midwest.

Since the railway shootings had begun, detectives had interviewed over 100 persons, but all the information obtained had proved quite useless, with one single exception. The snippet of information had seemed of little consequence at the time, but it proved to be the lead that would break the deadlock.

During the course of the investigations, Elkhart detective James Bowlby had been asking routine questions of an engine driver who had at one stage driven freight runs through Hammond, Indiana. The driver was a railwaymen's union official and because of this he had a good knowledge of the men employed on most of the area lines.

The driver recalled that on one trip his fireman had mentioned, as they were running through the Indiana Harbor Belt Depot yards, that a double murder had occurred there some years previously in which an engine driver and his fireman were shot. He asked the driver whether he knew of this, to which he had replied that he had heard something about it but that it was before his time as a railwayman. The fireman seemed to want to continue talking about it, but the driver merely shrugged the matter off. He particularly remembered that the fireman seemed quite put out that the driver wanted to drop the subject, and lapsed into a sulk. He added that the fireman was 'an odd fella' who used to talk to himself but was less inclined to talk to his fellow employees, being a rather taciturn man in company. His name, the driver said, was Rudy Bladel.

The detectives now looked into Rudy Bladel's background as a railway employee. After serving in the Korean war, he joined the Rock Island and Pacific Railroad Company, working out of Niles, Michigan. His father had worked for the same company before him, from the depot in Chicago.

In 1959, the Rock Island and Pacific had to change with the times much as other railway companies had to do. They had to open new stations and close others, lay new track and reroute many of their old established lines. The changes involved moving the centre of the company's railway operations from Niles, Michigan, to Elkhart, Indiana. The news was a bitter blow for Niles railwaymen – family men who had been born in the town and married and raised their children there, and depended on the local railway for their livelihood. A few of the more mobile workers moved to Elkhart, but they were the minority. Most of the men were laid off, and their union could do little about it. The best the company could come up with was to guarantee that half of the new Elkhart-based jobs would go to Niles men, the other half being available to local workers. Rudy Bladel was laid off and then re-employed at a lower rank in the Elkhart yards; this rankled, in the light of his excellent record of employment. He took it as a personal insult that he had been let go in favor of a man from another yard and then demoted to an inferior rank. He brooded over the situation and became more and more withdrawn, seldom talking to his fellow workers, but frequently muttering to himself.

In 1971, Bladel had got into a fight with one of his fellow workers in the Elkhart goods yard. The other man, an engine driver, was seriously wounded, Bladel less so. Both were taken to hospital in Elkhart, and when the driver asked Bladel outright why he had attacked him without provocation, he would not give him a straight answer but muttered under his breath something about 'railwaymen from Niles, Michigan'.

Bladel was charged with aggravated battery, to which he pleaded guilty, which earned him a sentence of one to five years in the state penitentiary. With good conduct in prison, he was released after having served only eighteen months of his sentence. At no stage, either in court, in prison or after his release, did he ever express regret, or explain the reason for his unprovoked attack on the engine driver.

In 1973 Rudy Bladel found himself free once more, but without a job to return to. On his conviction the Rock Island and Pacific had dismissed him, and without doubt Bladel, with his hitherto unblemished work record, felt this much more keenly than his spell in jail. The first thing he did immediately upon his release was to file an appeal for reinstatement in his old job, but this was rejected out of hand. It is little wonder that Rudy Bladel harboured such bitter feelings, albeit this was not a legitimate excuse to shoot seven of his fellow-workers.

The chief of police in Elkhart may have had his suspicions, but he had no proof that Rudy Bladel had been the man who had committed the murders. The most he could do was to order a surveillance to be put on Bladel. In 1978, in January – a year before the New Year's Eve murders – Bladel was seen entering a gunsmith's establishment in South Bend, Indiana, where he purchased a .357 Magnum. This was a clear violation of federal law, which provides that no ex-convict may own or possess firearms, and the FBI were notified. Bladel was arrested and sent to prison. The five-year sentence was cut to only eleven months by good behavior, and he was once again a free man – unfortunately for the New Year's Eve victims in Jackson, Michigan.

This time the chief of police at Elkhart lost no time in

putting out an alert for Rudy Bladel. He was arrested early
on New Year's Day as he stood in a queue to buy a ticket
home in the Jackson bus terminal. In his hand he carried a
copy of the morning local newspaper with the story of the
shootings. When searched, Bladel had no weapon on him,
and for the next forty-eight hours he exercised his right to
remain mute. Since it was known that Bladel had spent
the night of New Year's Eve in a local hotel, detectives
were deployed to look there for the murder weapon. It
was nowhere to be found in his hastily vacated hotel
room, so the officers instigated a thorough search of the
area, checking garbage bins, skips and landfill sites,
disused buildings and even the railway yards, before
moving further out to the wooded areas close to the town,
but without success.

The feelings of the police chief may be more easily
conjectured than described as he was forced to let his
suspect go because of a complete lack of evidence. There
was just no legal loophole under which he could be held
in custody pending the finding of the murder weapon and
ballistic comparison with the shell casings they already
had. The walking time-bomb was loose on the streets
again ...

Three months later, hikers trekking in the Cascade Falls
National Park not far from Jackson came across the broken
parts of a shotgun half-buried under some brushwood.
They took the pieces to the police. The officers lost no time
in tracing the gun, a Remington twelve-bore – by its worn,
but still visible, serial numbers. They were not unduly
surprised to discover that the gun had been registered to
Rudy Bladel. Immediately, the gun was put in working
order and a test firing carried out. Ballistics experts made a
comparison of the test-fired shells with those that had
been found on the railway freight yard platform in
Jackson. They matched. The gun had been the weapon
which had killed the three men on New Year's Eve.

Within the hour, a warrant for the arrest of Rudy Bladel
was issued, charging him with three counts of murder in
the first degree. A few hours later Bladel was spotted as he
cycled to his lodgings – a hostel for vagrants in Elkhart.
On 22 March 1979 he was booked into the town jail and

continued to remain silent as he was read his rights. A judge arranged a court-appointed attorney for him, since he was unemployed and without means.

At his trial six months later, Jackson County prosecutor Edward Grant produced what purported to be a signed confession, but Bladel stated that the police had forced the confession out of him under duress. The prosecutor then pointed out that the shotgun had been proved to be the murder weapon.

To this point, Bladel calmly replied that, although he could not deny that he had indeed once owned the gun which had been traced to him, he had sold it to a man whose name he had forgotten a few months before the murders. He had met the man in a tavern, he stated, adding that even if he could remember the man's name it might not be his real one. All this prevarication, however, failed to save Bladel from the sentence imposed by the judge on 29 August 1979 – three consecutive life terms in the state prison.

Rudy Bladel, though a man of few words, was not lacking in determination when it came to appealing his conviction, and after a great deal of protracted legal negotiation, the Michigan Supreme Court, in 1985, reversed the convictions, on the grounds that the confession which the police had produced in evidence had been obtained before the accused had had a chance to talk to his attorney and was therefore inadmissible as evidence.

Railwaymen in the area were apprehensive that Rudy Bladel might walk out of court a free man, but their fears were unfounded. The Jackson County prosecutor was not going to take any chances. He immediately filed his own appeal with the US Supreme Court, asking that Bladel be kept in custody pending the outcome. The request was granted, and the workers on the freight trains of Michigan and Indiana heaved sighs of relief.

The decision took a year to come through. On 1 April 1986 the US Supreme Court pronounced their ruling. They agreed with the decision of the State of Michigan that Bladel had been wrongly convicted and deserved a new trial. This was to be held in a different venue, and Bladel was to remain in custody until that time.

The new trial was scheduled to take place on 19 June 1987 in Kalamazoo, Michigan, and was little more than a rerun of the earlier proceedings, except that the confession was not put into evidence. The shotgun which had been the murder weapon was produced in court together with a number of slides showing the ballistic experts' findings. These included not only the matching of the shell cases from the test-firing with those found at the scene of the shootings, but also the presence of fibres in the breech of the gun which exactly matched similar fibres inside the suitcase Bladel had used to carry the gun.

The jury needed only two hours to reach their verdict. Rudy Bladel was again found guilty of the three Jackson murders, and was again sentenced to three consecutive life terms in the state penitentiary.

No amount of good behavior in prison will earn him any remission this time.

3

Murder at the YWCA

Patrick Byrne (1959)

Christmas was always an exciting time – at least for those who had families. Most of the girls who lived at the YWCA hostel in Birmingham had families to go home to for Christmas, but the odd few who did not had decided to make the best of a bad job and have as much fun as they could. So they set to and decorated the common room with holly, kept a log fire going, and laboriously glued together paper chains and streamers which they somehow managed to suspend from the high ceiling of the old Georgian house by standing on chairs and tables to reach the rafters. A Christmas tree was hauled in from the nearby market by four of the girls, two at each end, and soon the 12 ft. tree stood in a corner of the common room, resplendent in the tinsel, silver streamers, coloured balls and fairy lights for which they had all clubbed together. By the early evening of Wednesday, 23 December 1959, the room was ready for the coming festivities.

Most of the girls who were going home to spend Christmas with their families had already gone, but a few were still preparing for their departure the following day. One such girl was 20-year-old Margaret Brown, an office worker like the majority of the YWCA's residents. She was a Scot from Edinburgh and was greatly looking forward to the prospect of being reunited with her parents, brother and sister. In the hostel's laundry room she was pressing the dress she intended wearing for her trip, with her back to the door and the ironing-board before her. Suddenly the light went out. Since it was 7.45 p.m., it was dark. Had a fuse blown?

Margaret turned round just in time to see the shadowy form of a man come up behind her, one arm raised above his head. She screamed and moved away, but too late to avoid being hit on the head by a brick which the man was carrying in his hand. Still screaming, Margaret fell to the floor, and the last thing she remembered before losing consciousness was seeing the dark shadowy form dash out of the door, and hearing his retreating footsteps.

A girl came running into the room and switched on the light. When she saw Margaret Brown lying on the floor with her head in a pool of blood, she, too, began screaming. Other residents who had been in the common room watching TV came running into the room. They did not scream, but took the more practical steps of calling police and an ambulance.

A resident who had been in the backyard told police:

I saw a man in the yard. I saw him go into the building through the back door. He looked as though he was carrying something in his hand, but I could not see what it was. I thought he was a relative of one of the girls paying her a visit before Christmas, so I thought nothing of it.

The girl then went on to describe the intruder:

He was about 5ft. 7in. tall and stockily built, with curly light brown hair. He was youngish and had a sort of ruddy complexion. He was wearing a brown jacket, but I could not see what colour the rest of his clothes were.

Asked how she could give such a good description of the man although it was dark, the girl told police that an outside light is kept on so that residents can see where the rear entrance to the hostel is.

As Margaret Brown was taken to hospital, police put out an alert for the prowler, and in the meantime they instituted a search of the hostel. They found that most of the bedsitting-rooms were empty, since most of the girls had by now gone home to their families for the holiday. The rooms of the residents still at the hostel were unlocked; most had been in the common room watching TV. Room 4, however, quite near the end of the landing and easily accessible from the laundry room, was locked. When there was no reply to their pounding on the door, one of the officers asked another resident whose room No. 4 was and where the occupant was. He was told that the resident was Stephanie Baird, aged 29, the oldest of the girls living at the hostel. She was a native of Bishop's Cleeve, a village near Cheltenham in Gloucestershire, and was a typist, though temporarily unemployed. Asked where she was, the officers were informed that the last they had seen of her was when she had told them she was going to her room to pack her suitcase ready to leave the next morning to go home to her parents for the holiday. As far as they knew, she was still there.

She was, indeed, still there. When two policemen broke down the door they found her. Her decapitated body lay in a welter of blood on the floor; her head lay on the bed, staring up at the ceiling with sightless eyes from a pool of blood. The body, which was only partly clothed, had been subjected to horrific mutilations. Her breasts had been savagely bitten and bruised, and she had been raped with such violence that the pathologist who carried out the post mortem later stated that he had never previously seen such severe internal injuries caused in this way. The handle of a table knife lay on the bed beside the severed head, its broken blade, razor-sharp, having fallen to the floor near the body.

On top of a chest of drawers by the wall, a crumpled envelope lay, on which was written in an almost illiterate hand, 'This was the Thing I Tought would never come.'

The window of the room was wide open and had obviously been the killer's means of escape; the victim would not have had it open to such an extent on a cold December night. The window led on to the backyard and was only a short drop to the ground. No one had seen him leave, and the police realized immediately that a homicidal maniac was now loose in their midst. If such a man could break into a building occupied by at least seven or eight people, there was no telling what he would be prepared to do in his quest for another victim. It was the detectives' considered opinion, however, that he had attacked Margaret Brown only because he thought she had seen him clearly, which she had not, in order to silence her. Since he fled the building after his attack on Margaret Brown, it seemed apparent that he had killed Stephanie Baird before he had encountered Margaret in the laundry room.

Under the command of Detective Chief Superintendent James Haughton, the police now concentrated on an all-out hunt for the killer. Roadblocks were set up on every route out of Birmingham. Since it was obvious that the assailant must have become covered in blood, and that he would have had no time to wash even his hands after making such a hasty exit from the YWCA building, police officers were detailed to stop all motorists heading out of the area and ask to examine their hands. A few motorists demurred; some thought it a huge joke. 'Just like kids coming home from school – show your hands, boy!' one is reported to have said when interviewed by a newspaperman.

In the event, when the killer was apprehended, it was found that all this had been an unnecessary exercise, since the man did not drive or own a car. The police, however, were nothing if not thorough with such a psychopath loose on the streets, and they could not afford to take any chances.

While all this was going on, the Home Office pathologist, Dr T.D.E. Griffiths, was making his preliminary examination of the victim's body before it was taken away for autopsy. He stated that she had been strangled before being decapitated, and that the various horrendous injuries already referred to had been inflicted both before and after death. The fingerprint technicians who had dusted the scene of crime reported that they had been unable to raise any legible prints. The window which had been used both as entry and exit by the killer was found to have a faulty catch and would have been easily opened from the outside, but no prints were found on any part of it. Subsequent examination of the note found on the chest of drawers were also revealed no fingerprints. Even the knife the killer had used had been wiped clean.

Throughout the remainder of the evening, squads of police officers visited lodging-houses, pubs and amusement arcades in the area, asking questions and interviewing hundreds of people. A few were taken in for questioning at the police station, but all were eliminated and released.

The following morning – Christmas Eve – DCS Haughton ordered the manhunt to be extended to cover the entire city, whose population at that time was 1,100,000. The police found the holiday weekend extremely frustrating; no newspapers were published, and many people were out of town for the holiday. Radio and television were the only means of broadcasting appeals for information, but no one came forward with any useful lead.

After the holiday, on Sunday, 27 December, a young woman named Evelyn Peake presented herself at police headquarters. She told DCS Haughton that she had been out of the area over the holiday period, and had only just returned, when she had heard about the murder where she worked as a barmaid at the Welcome Inn, a pub only about 250 yards from the YWCA. The murder was practically the only topic of conversation at the pub.

She told DCS Haughton that on the night of the murder she had alighted from a bus in Wheeley's Road, near the YWCA hostel, at about a quarter to eight, when she saw a young man sitting on the pavement, slumped against the wall of a house almost opposite the bus stop. At first she thought he was just a drunk, but on looking at him more closely by the light of a street lamp she saw that he appeared to be injured in some way. She called to two men who were also leaving the bus to come to his assistance. One of these two men addressed the injured man: 'Blimey, mate – what have you been doing? Been in a fight?'

The young man looked up. His face was dirty, as though he had fallen in a garden. He was clutching a rolled-up dark-coloured plastic bag. 'I'll be all right when I can get on a bus,' he said, without volunteering how he had come by his apparent injuries.

The two men helped him to his feet, and as they reached the bus stop a bus came along and the young man lurched unsteadily on to it.

'Is this bus the one you want?' he was asked.

'Any will do,' had been his reply.

Haughton asked Miss Peake if she could describe the man.

'Well,' she said, 'he wasn't very tall – about five foot six, I should think. He had light-coloured curly hair – no hat or cap. It was too dark to see what colour his clothes were.'

'Did you notice any blood on his clothes?'

'It was too dark to see, but there might have been. If there was, I didn't notice any.'

Haughton next contacted the local bus depot, from which he learned that a number 8 Inner Circle bus left the Edgbaston terminus at 4.40 p.m. and arrived at the Wheeley's Road bus stop at 7.48 p.m. The dispatcher at the depot checked his records and was able to inform the superintendent that the conductor on that particular bus had been one William Humphreys.

The conductor was located, and related to Haughton that he did indeed remember the man in question. 'He got on my bus at the Wheeley's Road stop. He had blood on the front and sleeves of his jacket and his face was all dirty, like he had fallen into some mud. He reeked of alcohol, and I thought he'd been in a pub fight. He managed to get up on to the top deck.' Humphreys paused to think. 'About four rows from the front, I think his seat was. We had quite a few Christmas shoppers, mostly women. None of them would sit anywhere near him'.

'Can you describe this man?' Haughton asked.

'Well,' the conductor replied, 'he was about medium height, well-built, with fair curly hair. He didn't wear a hat or cap. He seemed to be in a sort of daze. When I asked him where he wanted to go, he didn't say anything, but just handed me a sixpenny piece, so I gave him a sixpenny ticket.'

'Can you remember where he got off?'

'At Hockley, I think.'

'Did you see which way he went?'

'No, but two other chaps got off at the same stop. Perhaps they might know, if you can find them.'

Haughton's next move was to send a detachment of forty officers to the Hockley area with orders to make a door-to-door search and question everybody, as well as keeping a lookout for the curly headed man. Then Haughton issued an appeal in the newspapers, on the radio and on television, for all persons who had been on the number 8 Inner Circle bus at the material times to come forward. After a day of ten hourly bulletins on the radio, ten persons came forward who had travelled on that particular bus, but they could add little to the bus conductor's description of the fair-haired passenger. All were agreed that he was drunk, seemed dazed, and looked as though he had been involved in a fight. But, they pointed out, he seemed to know where to get off – at Hockley – without any prompting, and managed to descend the stairs and alight from the bus unaided.

The two men who had got off the bus with him on the night in question did not come forward and could not be traced. According to the ticket record, there had been fifty people travelling on that bus at the time. That left thirty-nine passengers who had not come forward in response to the police appeal.

On the theory that some people travelled by that route every weekday evening at the same time, detectives were assigned to ride No. 8 Inner Circle double-decker for several consecutive nights and question all passengers. This threw up a few more who had been on the bus on the Wednesday night, but none of them could give the detectives any useful information. Several of them stated that they had not even seen the wanted man, being preoccupied with their Christmas purchases.

The house-to-house inquiries in Hockley had drawn a complete blank, and this aspect of the investigation was abandoned. Instead, Haughton now concentrated his attention on the theory that the man might have followed Stephanie Baird home after seeing her in the street. Inquiries of the residents remaining over the holiday

period at the hostel elicited the location of a ladies'
hairdressing establishment which Stephanie had visited,
keeping a four o'clock appointment, on the day of the
murder. She had had a shampoo and set, leaving the salon
at 5.30, saying she was going home as she had to prepare
for her trip the next day. The proprietress was able to
supply the police with details of what outdoor clothes
Stephanie had been wearing that day: a grey rubberized
raincoat with a mottled pattern and a green corduroy
collar, and a small matching hat which she wore on the
back of her head, held in place with hair-clips. These
articles were found in Stephanie's wardrobe in her room,
and a 26-year-old policewoman of the same height and
build as Stephanie was found to act as a lookalike for a
reconstruction. The policewoman bore a remarkable facial
resemblance to Stephanie, too. In the reconstruction,
people were asked to tell police if they had seen a girl who
resembled her and wore similar clothing during the
afternoon in question, prior to her four o'clock hairdressing appointment and after 5.30 when she emerged from
the salon and returned to the hostel. It was not known
whether she had walked, or whether she had taken the
bus.

The reconstruction failed to jog anyone's memory, so
Haughton followed this up by having the policewoman
lookalike photographed wearing Stephanie's clothing,
superimposing Stephanie's face on the photograph, and
then arranging for this composite photograph to be
published in every newspaper that circulated in Birmingham. People who were in the Wheeley's Road area on the
day of the murder were particularly asked to come
forward if they had any information, however trivial.
What they might consider to be a matter of little or no
significance, might prove to be a vital lead. Unfortunately
all this activity drew only a blank.

In the meantime, other detectives were questioning the
Christmas residents of the YWCA for details about the
murdered girl which might prove helpful. They learned
that Stephanie had lived at the hostel for about a year, and
had held an office job until she had been made redundant
owing to staff changes about three months before the

murder. She was a shy, quiet girl who had never been known to go out with men and had no known boyfriends. She liked to keep herself to herself, reading in her room, sewing or knitting. 'A bit of a loner' was how one of the other residents described her. She did not even have any close girlfriends, but was polite and pleasant to her fellow YWCA members. Very occasionally, she went to the cinema, always alone. She had no financial problems as her father had left her a small income after his death. Her mother had remarried and lived in her home village of Bishop's Cleeve in Gloucestershire with her stepfather.

By this time Margaret Brown had been discharged from hospital, having recovered from her ordeal. The police arranged for her to look through a number of mugshots of local sex offenders, but she failed to pick out anyone resembling the man who had attacked her in the laundry room. This was, perhaps, not unreasonable, since it had been dark at the time of the attack and she had seen only a shadowy male form.

January 1960 drew to a close, with the police no nearer to apprehending the killer of Stephanie Baird. DCS Haughton held a conference, from which he and his colleagues were able to agree upon certain conclusions. First of all, they were almost certain that the killer was a local man, or at least lived locally; a stranger to the area would not have known the layout of the YWCA hostel building. Secondly, they were of the considered opinion that soon after the murder the man had left the area, perhaps to stay with a relative or friend until the hue and cry for the murderer had abated. Thirdly, the detectives thought that the man did not reside in Hockley at all, but lived much nearer to the Wheeley's Road area, which would have enabled him to vanish from sight quickly after the crime. At this stage, therefore, the injured man on the bus was now considered to have no connection with the murder, but was just a drunk who had come to blows with another fellow in a pub.

Acting on these conclusions, the detectives now instigated a second door-to-door canvass of the Wheeley's Road area, at the beginning of February. This time, the question was whether any resident who had lived at the house until Christmas 1959 had moved shortly afterwards. The detectives also visited firms and asked employers to check whether any employee had been working until Christmas and had then failed to return to work after the holiday. The task was a daunting one – the area was densely-populated and there were a good many factories and other work premises to visit.

On 8 February they were talking to the landlady of a lodging-house about half a mile from the YWCA. She told the detectives that there had been a young Irishman named Patrick Byrne staying at her house up until Christmas Eve. She said that he was 27, stockily built and of medium height, with fair curly hair. The two officers looked at one another. 'Can we see your register?' they asked her. She obligingly brought out the book, from which the officers noted that Patrick Byrne had given an address in Dublin.

'When did he leave your house?' the detectives asked.

'On Christmas Eve,' the landlady replied. 'He was a very quiet young man. He never seemed to have any friends, and seemed rather lonely. I invited him to come and have a drink and a mince pie with myself and my husband on Christmas Eve, and he said he would, but he never came. We thought this rather odd, so I went up to his room to see if he was ill, perhaps. The door was unlocked. I went in and found that he had taken all his clothes and belongings and moved out without giving me any notice.'

'Where did he work?' the detectives asked.

'Some kind of factory job,' she said, 'but I don't know where. He never told me. So long as he paid his rent on time, I never asked any questions.'

'Did he have any mail?' the officers continued.

'Just one letter every week. He said it was from his mother in Lancashire.'

'Lancashire? Can you remember where?'

'Yes – it was Warrington on the postmark. Every Friday, the letter used to arrive. It's the only mail he ever had as far as I can recall.'

The officers thanked her for her help. Reporting back to police headquarters, they appraised DCS Haughton of their findings. Haughton contacted the police in Dublin and asked them to check the address Patrick Byrne had given in the landlady's register. The address was a lodging-house for working men. Byrne had stayed there, but it was some considerable time previously. The description they had matched that of the wanted man.

The superintendent now followed up the Warrington lead. He told Warrington police to check on every family named Byrne in the town until he found a Patrick Byrne, aged 27, fitting the description of the fugitive, who had returned home just in time for Christmas.

Late that same evening – Monday, 8 February – the Warrington police called back. 'We've found your man,' they told the elated superintendent. 'His name is Patrick Joseph Byrne, 27, a native of Dublin, and fits your description. He's been staying with his widowed mother in Birchall Street here since he arrived late on the night of 23 December. His mother has told us that he came to spend Christmas with her and stayed on. We've got him here at the police station but haven't questioned him.'

'Just keep him in custody,' Haughton told them. 'We'll be there as soon as possible.'

Without more ado, Haughton and three other officers drove the seventy-five miles to Warrington, and escorted Patrick Byrne back in short order to Birmingham, where they questioned him at length. The quietly spoken suspect then made a statement, and as a result he was charged with the murder of Stephanie Baird at the YWCA on 23 December 1959. He was committed for trial at Birmingham Magistrates' Court on 11 February. Mr D. Emrys Morgan, prosecuting, alleged that the accused, on his way home from work on the day in question, went to the YWCA hostel and committed the crime with which he was charged. Morgan added that he had left his lodgings the same night and gone to his mother's home in Warrington, Lancashire, where he had been ever since with the apparent intention of staying there, since it was known that he had been looking for a job.

After being informed of the charge, the accused was asked by the magistrate, Mr James Millward, if he had anything to say. In a firm voice, Byrne replied, 'No, sir.'

At his trial for the murder of Stephanie Baird at the YWCA, Patrick Byrne pleaded not guilty by reason of diminished responsibility. The evidence against him was incontrovertible; samples of his handwriting matched that on the envelope he had left on the top of the chest of drawers in the victim's room, and he had given detectives details of the crime that only he could have known. The jury returned a verdict of guilty, and Byrne was sentenced to life imprisonment.

Given leave to appeal, Byrne lost no time in making his petition. At the High Court hearing of his appeal, a verdict of manslaughter was substituted for that of murder. It availed him nothing, however, since the life sentence remained unaltered.

4
'Let's Cook Granny!'
Marie Witte (1984)

Trail Creek is a small rural community of some few hundred people a few miles from Michigan City which, despite its name, is not in Michigan but in the state of Indiana. No one seems to know how it came to be so named. Trail Creek, however, is a name that derives from the rugged nature of the terrain – a sparsely populated community of remote tracks, sluggish creeks, isolated farms and homesteads.

In Trail Creek lived a 74-year-old widow named Elaine Witte. She was a woman of many sorrows. The first tragedy in her life occurred when her only son was shot dead in his own home, apparently as a result of an accident. His elder son had been toying with his father's gun when it went off, hitting his father in the back of the head. The boys were 17 and 14 at the time.

A few months later, the house in which Elaine Witte's son's widow and her two boys lived mysteriously burned to the ground. The cause of the fire was never clearly established, and the insurance company paid out a somewhat reduced claim on this account. Elaine Witte invited her daughter-in-law Marie with the two boys, Eric and John, to come and live with her until they found a new home. This might have worked on a temporary basis to tide them over, but the new home was not to be found within their budget and they did not want to live in a mobile home or trailer. So the arrangement gradually became a permanent one.

Unfortunately the situation deteriorated, since Elaine and her daughter-in-law did not get on at all well, and the boys were spoilt and unruly. John, the younger, was expelled from junior high for smoking pot and under-age drinking; the older boy dropped out of his school and made no real effort to find a job. Marie refused to discipline them and let them run wild, which caused a great deal of friction and dissension in the family. Elaine did not at all approve of her daughter-in-law's liberal attitudes to raising children. Then, much to her relief, Eric joined the US Navy and in late 1983 was sent to Great Lakes naval base in Illinois. John was still at home with his mother and grandmother.

In the early part of 1984 neighbours of the family, who had not seen Elaine for several days, asked Marie where she was, and was told that she had gone on a holiday visiting relatives. She was vague about where she had gone, and equally so about when she might return. In the spring of the same year Marie bought a motor caravan and left with John for California, where Eric had been recently posted. Elaine had still not returned to the house by that time.

The year dragged interminably on with no news of either Elaine or Marie and John. Neighbours thought it rather odd that no one should even come and keep the house in good order and the gardens tidy, but after all it was their house and they could do as they liked with it. It had not been put up for sale, so the neighbours thought that perhaps they would be returning at some time in the foreseeable future. One of Elaine's relatives who lived in a city in the East, however, became more and more concerned as her letters were unanswered and she was unable to reach her by telephone. On checking, she found that the telephone had been disconnected and the number unobtainable.

The relative decided to make the long journey to Trail Creek to see if she could find out what was going on. Arriving at the Witte house, she managed to gain entry, and was shocked to discover that all the furniture had been removed. Her letters were lying unopened in the mailbox to the house. She decided to go to the Michigan City police to see if they could offer any advice. They told her that the best way to trace Elaine would be to see the manager of her bank. Being an old age pensioner she would receive social security cheques which would be paid into her bank.

When the bank manager checked Elaine Witte's account, he was able to disclose that in January she had transferred her considerable deposit account into her current account, and the cash had been systematically withdrawn by means of a 'cashpoint' card machine. It seemed rather more than a coincidence that Marie's account had been augmented by more or less the same amount that had been withdrawn from Elaine's account, give or take a few dollars. In late April Marie's account had been closed, at about the same time that she had purchased the motor caravan and headed off with John to California.

The bank manager explained to Elaine's kinswoman that all these transactions were perfectly legal. He stated that neither Elaine nor Marie had left a forwarding address – again, there was no legal obligation on their part to do so.

Having thus come to a dead end at the bank, the woman returned to the police at Michigan City and conferred with them again. Sergeant Eugene Pierce suggested that it might be possible to trace the missing pair through the social security office, who could inform him where Elaine Witte's cheques were being sent. This information, while not disclosed to a private individual, would be available to the police in cases where there was suspicion of misappropriation or fraud.

The social security office came up with the information that Elaine Witte's cheques were being mailed c/o General Delivery in San Diego, California. When these cancelled cheques were located, they were found to have been endorsed by Marie Witte on behalf of her mother-in-law and cashed.

Pierce requested that the cheques be examined by a handwriting expert to determine whether Elaine Witte's signature had been forged. In early November the report came back from Larry Ziegler, a handwriting expert with the FBI. He stated that, in his opinion, the signatures purporting to be those of Elaine Witte were tracings from an original signature. That was enough to warrant charges of a federal offence – forgery and conspiracy to defraud – against Marie Witte and her son Eric, who had cashed the cheques through his naval account. The pair were quickly located and taken into custody in San Diego.

Marie was questioned as to the whereabouts of her mother-in-law, to which she replied that she did not know and did not care. Marie's sister Madeline, who lived in another rural community not far from Trail Creek, Indiana, was located by Sergeant Pierce and Detective Sergeant Arland Boyd of the Indiana State police, who had been looking for someone who could throw some light on the matter. When Madeline told them that she had no idea where Elaine Witte was and that she hadn't heard from Marie since she had left for California, the two officers told her frankly that they did not believe her. She could be charged as an accessory, they told her, if she withheld information or obstructed the police in carrying out their investigation. Madeline then volunteered to make a statement.

After being advised of her legal rights, Madeline said that she knew that Elaine Witte was dead, and that her grandson had shot her with a crossbow. Moreover, she continued, Marie's husband Paul had not been killed accidentally: he had been deliberately shot by his son Eric at his mother's bidding. She had wanted to kill him herself, the woman added, but 'she hadn't the guts.'

Madeline continued to describe in her statement how Paul Witte had at one time been seriously injured in a motorcycling accident and that his injuries had left him moody, irritable and bad-tempered. He had been abusive to his wife and sons, and naturally enough there had been bad feeling between them. Marie had threatened to divorce him, but he had warned her that he would not pay her alimony or child support.

In desperation, the statement continued, Marie hatched the plot to have Eric shoot his father in a purportedly accidental misfiring of the gun. She and John would swear that they had witnessed the event and that it was entirely inadvertent. It had taken place on 1 September 1981, shortly before noon, when Paul lay on a sofa drunk. Eric had shot him in the back of the head as he had turned over in his sleep.

The police now drew out Madeline on the subject of the death of Elaine Witte. She stated that somehow Elaine learned that someone was using her bank card to withdraw money from her account, and she had accused John. Actually it was not John but Marie who had been withrawing the money, and she became apprehensive when her mother-in-law told her that she was going to take a trip to the bank to find out what was going on. Marie had called her sister asking her to come to the house as she needed help.

When she arrived, Marie informed her that John had shot his grandmother with a crossbow. In the meantime, she had telephoned Eric and asked him what they should do with the body. Eric had told her to put it in the freezer until he could manage to get leave and come home, during which time he would figure out the best way of disposing of the corpse.

Marie told her, the statement continued, that she and John had spent three days chopping up the body with knives, a chisel, a hammer and an electric chain saw. Then the body parts were put into the freezer. Eric then managed to get an overnight pass and came home as fast as he could. He advised his mother to have a garbage disposal unit and a trash compactor installed. The flesh they could then get rid of via the disposal unit and the bones could be crushed in the compactor.

Marie duly purchased the appliances, but they were not equal to the job. Parts of the flesh became enmeshed in the disposal unit and burned out the motor. When they put the old lady's head in the compactor, the machine broke. Madeline admitted in her statement that the easiest way to dispose of the body might be to cook all the flesh and put it into freezer containers, just like cooking a stew for the freezer. The containers with their grisly contents could then be kept in the deep-freeze until Eric's next leave, when he could decide how to dispose of them, and also the bones, which would have to be frozen separately. Thus, taking up Madeline's idea, the family spent a week gradually reducing Elaine Witte's remains to manageable portions by cooking them on the same stove on which they cooked their food.

Boyd and Pierce, armed with Madeline's statement, now interviewed Eric and John. After being advised of his legal rights, John volunteered to make a statement. He said that he had never got on with his grandmother, who was always picking on him and accusing him of taking money from her purse. His mother had told him that Granny was going to the bank to check on some withdrawals from her bank account which someone had been making by using her cashpoint card. His mother had said that if the old lady found out what was going on, she would throw them all out of her house into the street. The only solution, she had said, was to get rid of her before she could do so.

John's statement continued that his mother had told him that Elaine planned to make the trip to the bank the next morning, so she had to be stopped before she could go. His mother awakened him at 6 a.m. the next day and told him that it was 'now or never' and that if he did not do something they would all be homeless. John stated that he went down to the basement where Eric kept a trunk with his belongings stored while he was in the Navy, which included a crossbow. He brought it upstairs, went to his grandmother's room and shot her in the chest as she slept. He then called to his mother and told her that the old lady was dead.

His mother's reply was to inform him that she had an appointment with the social security office in Chicago. While she was gone, she had told him, he was to clean up the blood as best he could and burn the bedding in the boiler. He said that he also took a garbage bin and put his grandmother's body head first into it, put on the lid and brought it downstairs. When he asked his mother why she had not suggested cutting up the body and burning it in the boiler, she had replied that the smell of burning flesh would alert neighbours.

The statement went on to describe the difficulty they

had had in cutting up the body for the freezer so that it would fit into the containers. Finally, his mother had purchased an electric chain saw to facilitate the job.

The detectives now interviewed Eric, whom they confronted with his brother's statement. Eric voluntarily gave the detectives an account of his involvemnt. He hadn't really wanted any part of it, because of the trouble he'd had after he had shot his father. He felt sure that the police would connect this later crime with that shooting.

Eric stated that after he had obtained leave and come home, he admitted that it had been his idea to instal a garbage disposal unit and a trash compactor. He had only an overnight pass, but promised to obtain a longer leave in another couple of weeks or so on compassionate grounds, saying that his mother was seriously ill. He managed to obtain two nights' leave and this time he brought with him a buddy from his ship to whom he confided the predicament the family had got itself into. Not until his buddy had spent a couple of nights at the house, however, did he tell him that his grandmother's body, not-so-neatly dismembered and cooked, was in the deep-freeze. He told him that John had accidentally shot the old lady when he stumbled as he was carrying the crossbow upstairs.

Eric had purchased some acid, his statement continued, but it was useless for the purpose he had in mind – to dissolve the bones to facilitate their disposal. So they smashed them up as best they could with a hammer, including the head, pulling out all the teeth with pliers to avoid identification.

Eric's buddy offered the perfect solution to the disposal of the body parts, Eric's statement continued. Since they were due to leave the training camp and take up a posting in San Diego, they could drive to California and throw the frozen containers of body parts out at various isolated places along the route, and if anyone found them they would be unrecognisable as human body parts. In the meantime Marie had purchased an old second-hand pick-up truck with a camper trailer, which she grandly called a motor caravan.

And so the grisly disposal took place, across three states, and hardened policemen winced as Eric described in detail the exploits of his callous family.

Eric's buddy gave a statement confirming all that Eric had told police, and was charged with illegally disposing of a human body. In exchange for a promise to testify against the murderers of Elaine Witte, he was given a seven-month jail sentence, having entered a plea of guilty as charged.

Eric himself was also offered immunity from prosecution in exchange for his testimony regarding the murder of Elaine Witte, but his immunity did not extend to the murder of his father in the previous shooting. For that he received a twenty-year sentence, and is currently serving in prison.

John was charged with involuntary manslaughter, to which he pleaded guilty in a plea-bargaining deal whereby he agreed to testify against his mother in exchange for the reduced sentence of twenty years in prison.

Marie Witte was charged with first-degree murder and with conspiracy to murder, but she was not extradited to Indiana until after she and Eric had stood trial for the federal forgery charges in California. Both she and Eric were convicted, but sentencing was delayed until after the conclusion of the trials for the murders of Elaine and Paul Witte in Indiana.

The trial of Marie Witte for the murder of her mother-in-law commenced on 4 November 1985 in Michigan City before Judge Donald de Martin. The prosecutor was William Herbach, while Marie was represented by Scott King, a local attorney.

The first witness to be called was Marie's sister Madeline. Her testimony repeated the statement she had made earlier to the police. She confirmed her knowledge of the fact that Marie had made an unsuccessful attempt to poison her husband previous to having intimidated her elder son Eric to shoot his father. Finally, she related to a hushed court in chilling detail how she and her sister had spent almost a week cooking the flesh of Elaine Witte and filling freezer containers with the human stew. Two women in the public gallery and a male juror fainted and had to be carried out.

The judge ordered a recess until the unfortunate juror could recover sufficiently to return to the court, and he also told the spectators in the public gallery that if they were too squeamish to listen to the evidence, then perhaps they should leave the court. None did so, and the two women also returned. This, however, was not the only sensation that would be reported from the courtroom that day ...

John was the next witness. He related how his father had abused him, his brother and his mother. He stated that he was present in the room when his brother had shot his father, and that he had 'no feelings' about the murder, adding, 'He deserved all he got.' Regarding his grandmother's death, John stated that he had never got on with her, that she was constantly picking on him and accusing him of stealing from her. When he shot her, he said, he was merely carrying out his mother's orders.

On being cross-examined by Scott King, the attorney questioned John in such a manner as to imply that he had not shot her on his mother's instructions at all, but that it had been his own idea to kill her because of her accusations and the bad feeling between them. At this suggestion, John flared up, swore, and called the attorney a liar. When King persisted with his theory, John appeared that he was going to leave the witness-stand to strike the attorney, but he was restrained by a bailiff. The judge then ordered a recess until such time as the witness could control himself.

Eric was next called to the stand. He began his testimony by stating that he had received no immunity from prosecution for the murder of his father. He stated that his mother had come to him, bruised and sobbing, and saying that she could no longer stand the abuse and that he (Eric) 'must do something'. She told him that if he did not kill his father, she would kill herself. Faced with the choice of losing his father or his mother, he had agreed to shoot his father and make it look like an accident with the gun.

One day while he was at his naval training establishment he received a call from his mother to say that John had killed Granny and asking him to get leave urgently and come home at once to advise her what to do. He testified that the news had not been wholly unexpected, since he had been aware for some time of the bad feeling between his brother and the old lady. He told the court how he had managed to get overnight leave, and had advised his mother to install a garbage disposal unit and a trash compactor to dispose of the body.

Eric's naval buddy was the next witness. He recounted how he had been told that John had accidentally shot his grandmother in a mishap with a crossbow. Out of friendship for Eric, he had agreed to help dispose of the frozen body parts, in an effort to help and protect the family.

Prosecutor Herbach concluded the State's case with testimony from police investigators, forensic experts, and other witnesses who could add vital evidence. The staff of the bank where Elaine Witte had held her accounts testified how her savings had been transferred to her current account and then systematically withdrawn by means of her cashpoint card. Marie's account had been augmented by more or less the same amounts of money on the same dates. A store manager at the shop where Marie had purchased the garbage disposal unit and the trash compactor testified how she had insisted that the appliances be delivered and installed immediately.

When the State rested its case, Marie's attorney called her to the stand to testify in her own behalf. She told of how her husband Paul had changed after being involved in a motorcycling accident in which he had sustained serious head injuries. He would abuse both his sons, beat them, and beat her when she tried to defend them. If she refused him sex, he would tear off her clothes and rape her. She would frequently refuse to go out of the house after she had received black eyes and other bruising, to avoid being seen by neighbours.

One day, she testified, her son Eric had come out of the house to where she was sitting in the back garden, stating that he had shot his father. She was sure it had not been an accident with the gun, she stated, because she had heard them arguing, shouting and swearing. To protect her son, she concocted a story about a gunshot misfiring while the weapon was being cleaned and oiled ready for a game hunting expedition, and told John what to say when questioned by police.

Turning to the murder of Elaine Witte, the witness described the bad relationship between the deceased and her son John. She told how the old lady had called him 'a worthless bum' and accused him of stealing from her purse. She flatly denied any idea of killing the old lady or inciting her son to do so. She also testified that John had come to her saying that he had not intended to kill Granny but he had tripped and the crossbow he was carrying had fired.

Marie did not deny that she had helped dispose of the body by dismembering it with an electric chainsaw so that it could fit more easily into the deep-freeze. She also admitted enlisting the aid of her sister in cooking the remains so as to disguise them as a meat stew. Marie maintained throughout that she had done all these things only to protect John, because she realized that the police would remember that Eric had accidentally shot his father and now that John had accidentally shot his grandmother, they would put two and two together.

Marie also did not deny that she had withdrawn Elaine's money from the bank and putting it into her own account. She reasoned that if her mother-in-law was dead then she would have no use for the money, and she did not want it to go to less deserving relatives who never even visited the old lady for years at a time.

Under cross-examination, Prosecutor Herbach asked Marie to explain the difference in her story from that which her two sons had testified to. She replied that she could not explain this. 'I have always been good to both of them,' she replied. 'Now they have turned against me. Don't ask me why. I don't know.'

In his closing speech, Herbach pointed out that the accused had freely admitted her part in disposing of the body, but the point the jury had to consider was whether she had influenced and conspired with her son to kill her mother-in-law. What it all boiled down to was, in essence, whether they would believe her story, or whether they would believe the version given by her sons and her sister

Madeline. Pointing to Marie, he said: 'Look at her. She is a scheming and greedy woman. She used her own sons to kill her husband and her mother-in-law because, on her own admission, she 'hadn't the guts' to do it herself.'

After Judge de Martin gave his final charge to the jury, they retired during the afternoon of Friday, 8 November, and at 7 p.m. they sent word that they had reached a unanimous verdict. The accused had been found guilty on both charges – first-degree murder and conspiracy to murder. When the verdict was read out in court, Marie gave no outward sign of emotion. She was sentenced to sixty years in prison for murder and fifty years for the conspiracy charge, to be served consecutively. In effect, this means that she will remain in prison for the remainder of her life without possibility of parole.

Marie Witte will have 110 years in which to think about what she has done – if she lives that long.

5
Murder on the A34

Raymond Leslie Morris (1969)

Of murders unspeakable, the most unspeakable of all must be the rape-slaying of a little girl, and it is when the police are conducting an all-out manhunt for such a killer that they put out their greatest efforts, stretching themselves to the limit and leaving quite literally no stone unturned.

One of the greatest hunts for a missing child in British police history was the search for 7-year-old Christine Darby, who had disappeared while playing outside her home on the afternoon of Saturday, 19 August 1967. Christine had received permission from her mother to go out to play with two small friends, 8-year-old Nicholas Baldry and another little boy of the same age, Alwyn Isaacs, whose parents were from Jamaica, Alwyn having been born in Britain.

The three playmates called round the block from Christine's terraced home in Camden Street, Walsall, Staffs. Along the way they called at various houses to see whether some of their other neighbourhood friends would come out and join them. None could, so the three walked slowly back towards Camden Street, trying to decide what game to play. It was a warm and sunny afternoon, and there were many exciting games that could be played out of doors. Who would want to stay in on a day like this?

A few yards from the junction of Camden Street with

Corporation Street, a light-coloured car pulled up by the kerb alongside the children. The driver opened the passenger door and asked for directions to Caldmore Green. He pronounced 'Caldmore' as 'Karmer' in the local dialect. The children pointed out the right direction, but the man asked Christine, who was dressed in dark blue denim jeans, a white T-shirt and black plimsolls, to 'hop in and show him the way'. Christine, impishly pretty with her straight dark hair cut in a fringe and her quick, friendly smile, readily agreed. In those days there was little opportunity for car rides among the children of working people, so it was easy to tempt such a child with this kind of offer.

The boys watched Christine get into the car, which she did perfectly willingly. They watched from the pavement as the car moved off after reversing into Corporation Street, but, to their astonishment, the driver turned left instead of right – the opposite way to that which the children had clearly pointed out for Caldmore Green. They were suspicious immediately, and thought that Christine had been 'kidnapped', and Nicholas ran straightaway to Christine's home to tell Mrs Lilian Darby. Before three o'clock – less than an hour after Christine had gone out to play – the police had been called and were already swinging into action.

The Walsall division set up road blocks immediately, and the police forces of neighbouring districts were alerted. Assistant Chief Constable Gerald Baumber of the West Midlands police instigated an intensive inquiry in the Camden Street area, while the Staffordshire County force concentrated on Cannock Chase, the vast tract of commonland, woodland and scrub nearby. No fewer than 500 police officers with fifty tracker dogs, as well as 250 soldiers and airmen, began a systematic search of the Chase inch by inch. The Chase is eighty square miles in area.

The following day PC Arthur Ellis, a mounted policeman attached to the Staffordshire County headquarters, was riding his horse through the Chase about two miles north of Cannock when he spotted a pair of child's knickers hanging on the branch of a fallen tree. These, shown to Christine's grandmother, Mrs Henrietta Darby, were immediately identified as Christine's. Mrs Darby was able to recognise them by a particular kind of cotton she had used to mend them. Later the same day a forestry sub-contractor, James Leach, found a child's plimsoll off the main Penkridge Road, which runs across Cannock Chase. This, too, was subsequently identified as Christine's by her mother, who had marked the plimsolls with the initials C.D. and the date of purchase.

On Monday, 21 August, no sign of Christine having been found, Arthur Rose, Chief Constable of Staffordshire County police, called in Scotland Yard for assistance. Speaking to Assistant Commissioner Peter Brodie, Rose said that he had no doubt that he had another child murder on his hands, and that he would need all the help he could get. Within the previous two years two other small girls had been found in the same general area, murdered by suffocation and sexually assaulted, and buried together in a makeshift grave on Cannock Chase. Their killer had never been found.

It was in January 1966 that the two pathetic little bodies had been found in a lonely part of the Chase called Mansty Gully. Diane Joy Tift, 5, who, like Christine Darby, had also lived in Walsall, had been missing for two weeks. Like Christine, she, too, had vanished close to her home in the late afternoon of 30 December 1965. Margaret Reynolds, six years old, whose decomposed body was found at the bottom of the grave with the body of the other child lying over it, had vanished on 8 September that same year, some time in the early afternoon after leaving home to return to afternoon school. She never arrived. Margaret lived in Aston, a suburb of Birmingham.

Despite the early calling in of Scotland Yard's Murder Squad, who worked intensively on the case for more than five months, all their efforts were unavailing, and no suspect was ever apprehended. It seemed obvious to the police that the two murders must have been the work of one man, because of his having buried the later victim in the same grave as the earlier one; they also thought that he was probably a local man with some knowledge of the area. Beyond this they had no clue, and the length of time that had elapsed before the finding of the bodies was against them.

At the inquest on the two little girls, the Coroner, Mr K.T. Braine-Hartnell, warned parents: 'This repugnant pervert is still at large. Children in this area should not run about unaccompanied. While this murderer is at large no child is safe.'

As the months passed and 1966 gave way to 1967, the tragedy of Diane and Margaret faded from the minds of parents. No longer did little grim-faced groups of men and women huddle together on street corners, in pubs, outside school playgrounds. Vigilance slackened. After all, the children could not be kept cooped up indoors all the time: they had to go out into the fresh air to play sometimes. And for many of these youngsters from the tiny terraced houses which had no gardens, that meant the street outside, or the park. If any of the parents had any misgivings about the possibility of men with abnormal urges still lurking in the area, they quickly stifled them with that misguided old saying, 'It couldn't happen to *my* child.'

Until now.

On the fourth day after little Christine had been reported missing, her body was found, covered hastily with bracken and twigs, on Cannock Chase. One hour later Detective Inspector (later Deputy Assistant Commissioner) Ian Forbes, together with Detective Sergeant Tom Parry, arrived from Scotland Yard: they were already on their way before Christine was found. As they stood at the spot and saw the child's pathetic ravaged body, lying on her back as she had died, arms outflung, with legs apart and knees drawn up, *sans* underclothing, Tom Parry uttered in a choked voice: 'My God, guv'nor, that could have been my little girl. We just have to find the bastard that did this.'

It was action rather than words that would catch the killer. Strenuous efforts were made to trace every person who had been on Cannock Chase during the previous four days. These inquiries took up a great deal of valuable time without leading to the murderer. Then 24,000 leaflets were printed for distribution to the public. A photograph of Christine bore the caption: 'Were you on Cannock Chase on Saturday, 19 August after 2.30 p.m.?' On the reverse side was a map of the area. All roads leading to the Chase were manned by uniformed police officers, and all car drivers were stopped and questioned.

The police were convinced that the murderer was a local man, from his pronunciation of 'Caldmore' as 'Karmer'. The boy witness who had alerted Christine's mother to the 'kidnapping' was positive about that. Unfortunately he had been unable to take the number of the car, or be more precise about its description than that it was of a 'light' colour. Now, as the investigation progressed, several people came forward to volunteer information. A Mr Clive Hodgson of Walsall stated that he had seen a grey car, which he thought could have been an Austin Cambridge, drive past his house at about 2.45 p.m. on the day Christine disappeared. In the passenger seat, Mr Hodgson stated, was a small girl of Christine's general description, who 'appeared to be in a panic, turning round all the time'.

Another witness, Miss Kathleen Harbridge, of Rushall, said that she saw a gray car driven by a man with a small girl in the passenger seat who had both hands to her mouth and 'a frightened look on her face'. A Mr and Mrs Greenall, of Waltham Abbey, were travelling near Cannock in their car when they saw a grey Austin Cambridge with a child in the passenger seat who 'seemed to be crying and trying to open the door'. Another witness, Mrs Sadie Mansfield, of Cannock, said that she saw a similar grey car with a child passenger who was 'standing up close against the passenger door'.

Another group of witnesses had observed such a car on the Chase and, though some of them could give quite a detailed description of the driver, they stated that there was no child with him at that particular time. Among these witnesses a Mr Victor Whitehouse, of Hednesford, was walking his dog along one of the woodland paths on the Chase when he observed a man standing beside a grey car – possibly an Austin A60 – which had been backed into a narrow opening and was in fact partly concealed by a fallen tree. Mr Whitehouse particularly remembered the incident because he knew that the area was prohibited to vehicles by the Forestry Commission, and he was therefore surprised to see a car there.

A Mrs Jeanne Rawlings, of Wolverhampton, also saw a grey Austin on the Chase and was able to give the police almost as good a description of the driver as Mr Whitehouse had been able to do. The police were able eventually to put together a good Identikit photograph from these two descriptions. The car was almost certainly an Austin A55 or A60, and this knowledge helped to narrow the field considerably by eliminating cars of other makes.

No fewer than 25,000 car owners were investigated and eliminated from the inquiry. The police also examined 1,375,000 vehicle taxation files – a stupendous and time-consuming task indeed – and in addition to all this they interviewed 80,000 people in the area. Not content with this painstaking legwork, they also traced owners of gray Austin A55s and A60s who had gone abroad to Eire, Malta, Spain, Germany, Italy, Libya, the Gambia, Nigeria, Ghana, South Africa, Canada, Singapore and Australia.

During the first five weeks of these intensive inquiries the police worked a shift system round the clock. This was in the first instance necessitated because the vast majority of the thousands of people interviewed were at work in the daytime and were more likely to be available for interview in the evening. More than 28,000 men between the ages of 21 and 50 were interviewed and eliminated from the inquiry. Most were very co-operative; public feeling was very strongly aroused by this third child murder in the area in less than two years. In all, 184,606 people were interviewed by just 134 officers – a Herculean task. Yet all this effort failed to flush out the killer.

The police now worked out the most likely theories based on the information already in their files. The A34 linked all the places where the children had lived – Aston (Margaret Reynolds), Bloxwich and Walsall, where Diane Tift had successively lived, and Cannock, where all three bodies had been found. The total distance involved was just under 17 miles.

It seemed quite feasible, too, that there was a link with

an earlier, still unsolved crime. Julia Taylor, 9, had been enticed into a car near her home in Bloxwich on 1 December 1964. She was driven through Walsall to an isolated spot where the driver sexually assaulted her and attempted to strangle her, finally throwing her out of the car through a gap in a hedge and leaving her for dead. Soon afterwards she was found by a passer-by, who rushed her to hospital in his car, where she recovered, and later was able to show the police the route over which she had been driven. She remembered that at one point she had asked the driver where they were, and he had replied 'Bentley', again indicating a man familiar with the area, since Bentley is a small suburb of Walsall that a stranger would be unlikely to know.

Just as the police were certain that the killer was a local man, so, too, did they fear that unless he was caught quickly he would strike again. They were right on both counts. It was because he tried to entice another small girl into his car that he was finally traced and caught. The new vigilance of Midlands parents, prompted by the frighteningly indelible impression that this third child murder in their midst had made upon them, was a direct cause of the quick-witted awareness of one Walsall woman whose presence of mind was to prove the eventual downfall of the killer.

During the early evening of 4 November 1968 a 10-year-old girl named Margaret Aulton was playing alone on some waste ground at the corner of Queen Street and Bridgeman Street in Walsall. In the forecourt of a garage opposite a man sitting in his car watched the child as she put the finishing touches to a bonfire ready for Guy Fawkes's Night. The driver of the car left his vehicle and walked across to her, asking her whether she would like any Catherine wheels or rockets which he had in his car. What 10-year-old would not be intrigued? So she walked with him over to the car. Opening the passenger door, he said, 'The fireworks are over there.' Margaret could not see any fireworks, so she decided to go back to her bonfire, but as she attempted to do so the man grabbed her by the arm and tried to push her into the car. Margaret, however, was quite a strong little girl for her age and managed to break away. He started after her and, just at that moment, a Mrs Wendy Lane, a neighbour who knew Margaret, emerged from a fish-and-chip shop in Bridgeman Street and saw them. She did not recognize the man, who as soon as he realized that he had been seen, jumped into his car and drove off at speed. Mrs Lane identified the car as a green-and-white Ford Corsair, and had been quick enough off the mark to make a correct mental note of its registration number.

As well as saving this little girl from almost certain sexual assault, if not murder, Mrs Lane's prompt action led directly to the killer of Christine Darby. The car was quickly traced to one Raymond Leslie Morris, a 39-year-old works foreman, who lived with his second wife Carol in a fourth-floor council flat in Regent House, Green Lane, Walsall – just opposite the police station!

It transpired that Morris had already been interviewed more than once. In December 1964 he was questioned by detectives investigating the assault on Julia Taylor. Four witnesses had seen a two-tone Vauxhall car fitted with a hand-operated spotlamp at the place where Julia was found. At that time Morris owned such a car, but gave an alibi for the date and time in question which was confirmed by his wife. Morris vehemently denied all knowledge of the attack, and the case remained unsolved on police files.

Morris had also come to the notice of the police in October 1966 when a complaint was made against him regarding indecent assaults on two girls aged 10 and 11. According to their accounts, Morris had taken them to his flat during his lunch hour, persuaded them to disrobe, and induced them to photograph him with each child in turn, using a Polaroid camera with a delayed-action device. He then gave them each two shillings, and told them not to tell anyone.

Several weeks later one of the girls told her parents, who informed the police. Morris was interviewed, but denied the allegations. His flat was searched, and although photographic equipment was found, no photographs of an indecent nature were in evidence. The matter was submitted for legal advice, and no further action was taken, the girls' evidence having been uncorroborated.

The attempted abduction of Margaret Aulton involved a green-and-white Ford Corsair, but a check through the vehicle registration records showed that at the time of Christine Darby's murder Morris had owned a grey Austin A55 Cambridge. Perhaps Morris had good reason for constantly changing his car ...

During the course of Christine's murder investigations he was routinely interviewed, along with thousands of others, and given a questionnaire for completion. In this he stated that he had left work on Saturday, 19 August just after 1 p.m., arriving home just before two o'clock, and he'd then spent the afternoon with his wife looking round the shops in Walsall. His wife Carol confirmed this.

The officers saw him again three days later and asked him to describe his route home from work. His account did r.ot include either Camden Street or Caldmore Green.

By early the following year, as police suspicion was growing against Morris, it was decided to interview him a third time. The two officers whose job this was thought that he bore some resemblance to the Identikit photograph that had been released. Again they asked Morris to describe his route home from work, and again he gave them the same details as before. Once more his wife confirmed his alibi for the time he returned home, and it was impossible to shake her.

Morris's latest statement was now compared with his previous one, and it was found that, although the later account of his journey home from work was substantially the same as he had given previously, he had routed himself slightly farther away from the neighbourhood of Camden Street and Caldmore Green than in the preceding statement. Asked to explain the discrepancy, Morris replied simply that the slight difference was merely a question of memory after such a length of time. The police were becoming more and more certain in their own minds that this man knew more than he was admitting to them, but there was very little that they could do without positive proof. It was not until November of that year that their chance came, when he was apprehended for the attempted abduction of Margaret Aulton.

The little girl who had been lucky enough to escape

unharmed as she was preparing to enjoy her Guy Fawkes's Night celebrations had noticed that the driver of the car was wearing a silver watch and bracelet. This small detail did not mean a great deal at the time, but was to prove damning in later investigations.

After Morris's car was traced he was arrested and taken to the police station opposite his flat. The attempted abduction had taken place at 7.45 p.m., but Morris, who denied all knowledge of the incident, maintained that he had arrived home at 7.35 p.m. On this occasion, however, his wife did not substantiate his alibi. She said that he arrived home at 8 o'clock; she particularly remembered the time because 'Coronation Street' was just ending on TV. He could therefore easily have been at the spot where Mrs Lane saw him at 7.45 p.m.

Another interesting point emerged when the Walsall police officers accompanied Morris from his place of work to his home on 5 November to question him about the attempted abduction. At their request he drove them along the route he normally took when going home from work and, in contrast to his two statements about his route which he had made to them earlier, the route along which he drove them included both Camden Street and Caldmore Green.

For the next few days intensive inquiries were mounted into Morris's background. The police wanted to find proof, or anything that could be construed as corroborative evidence, that Morris could have killed Christine Darby. The inquiries uncovered the earlier assaults on the two girls aged 10 and 11, who were in fact related to his second wife Carol and it was for this reason that it had been decided not to proceed with the complaint at the time. The girls' mother decided never to leave them alone with Morris at any time, and had also noticed that he was always 'very interested' in little girls.

By 15 November 1968 the police had enough evidence to arrest Morris, which they did at 7.15 a.m. that day as he was on his way to work. When told that he was being detained in connection with the murder of Christine Darby, his first words were: 'Oh, God! Is it my wife?' In these six words he unwittingly revealed what the police had suspected all along – that the alibi his wife had given him was false.

Detective Inspector Forbes knew that Carol Morris was the key to the problem, but he still had to prove it. He had Detective Inspector Norman Williams search her flat, in her presence. A large number of photographs were found, some of them pornographic. These included several showing Morris indecently assaulting children, including Carol Morris's own five-year-old cousin in their flat. The pictures had all been taken by means of a delayed-action device. One of them showed a man's hand wearing a distinctive silver watch and bracelet, which was later identified by Margaret Aulton as the watch and bracelet Morris was wearing when he attempted to force her into his car on 4 November. Morris must have realized the vital importance of this watch as a clue, because when he was searched by the reception officer at Winson Green Prison after his arrest the watch was found round his ankle.

Forbes interviewed Carol Morris at Hednesford Police Station, where, under skilled interrogation, she eventually admitted that she had given a false alibi for her husband. After being shown the pictures which it was proved that her husband had taken in their own flat – sometimes when she was there in another room at the time – and after seeing the proof that even her own 5-year-old cousin was not safe from her husband's perverted attentions, Carol Morris became much more co-operative. Only then did she realise the full enormity of the character of the man she had married. She was fourteen years younger than her husband and to some extent she had been dominated by him.

By now Carol Morris was admitting that her husband, far from arriving home at two o'clock, had come in at about 4.30 p.m. Afterwards they had gone out, purchased some cakes from Marks and Spencer's in Walsall, and then driven to her mother's house. Carol's mother, Mrs Edith Pearse, told Forbes that Raymond had apologized for being late, saying that he had had to stay late at work. However, it was subsequently found that he had clocked off at 1.13 p.m., and that there was no truth in his explanation.

Morris appeared in February 1969 before Mr Justice Ashworth and a jury of nine men and three women. He pleaded not guilty to the murder of Christine Darby, not guilty to attempting to abduct Margaret Aulton, but guilty to assaulting the 5-year-old girl shown in the photographs. He was found guilty of Christine's murder, for which he received a life sentence. He was also given three years' imprisonment for the attempted abduction and one year for the indecent assault, the sentences to run concurrently.

After passing sentence, the judge said: 'There must be many mothers in Walsall and the area around whose hearts will beat more lightly as a result of this verdict. It must have been a nightmare for the mothers and fathers in Walsall over the last months when they heard that a child may be missing ... '

Forbes and other police officers involved have frequently been asked whether Morris was the killer of Margaret Reynolds and Diane Tift, or the abduction of Julia Taylor. Without voicing any private theories they may have had on the matter, they have always had to admit that they had no evidence linking Morris with these killings. It is significant, however, that since the Cannock Chase killer has been safely under lock and key, the parents of litle girls in the Walsall area no longer walk in fear.

6
Merry Christmas, Mom
John Graham (1956)

Floyd Wood was at the controls of a freight train of the Union Pacific railway bound for Denver, Colorado, when his nephew Roland Wood, who was the guard, called to him. 'Uncle,' he called. 'Look! There's a meteor in the sky!' Rushing into the cabin of the engine, he pointed out of the window. A shape, outlined in flame, was streaking through the sky at an incredible speed, then suddenly, as the two men watched, it catapulted to earth at a thirty-five-degree angle.

Almost by instinct, the two men looked at their watches. The time was 7.05 p.m. When they looked up again, clouds of smoke were billowing up into the sky from the point where the fiery object had hit the ground. Gradually the mushroom cloud turned pink and finally crimson with seething flames which shot up fifty feet or more. They could still see tongues of flame licking the night sky as the train pulled into the goods yard at Eastlake, twenty-five miles from Denver.

'Well, I'll be goddamned!' exclaimed Floyd as he brought the locomotive to a halt. 'That's no meteor! Never saw a meteor behave like that in my life!'

'Could it have been an explosion of some kind?' queried Roland. 'Point is, uncle – I never heard any bang.'

'Neither did I. You wouldn't anyway even if there was one – the engine was making such a racket it would drown out any sound.'

About thirty-five miles north of Denver, Bonnie Lang, who lived with her son Bud on a small farm, was washing the dishes in the kitchen of her farmhouse when she saw from the window a glaring light in the sky. She rushed out into the yard where Bud was tinkering with his car. 'What on earth ...?' she cried. Her sentence was unfinished as she and her son saw a large object, which appeared to be engulfed in flames, fall out of the sky and crash into a field about a mile from where they were standing with a tremendous bang. She was pelted with small particles of metal which felt hot. Grabbing Bud, she bundled him into the car and climbed in herself for protection as chunks of burning metal rained down from the sky all around them, narrowly missing the house. A metal bin containing plastic food trays thudded to the ground just in front of the gate. It was then that they realized that it had come from an airplane. When the bombardment had subsided Mrs Lang told her son to go in and call the fire service, the police and the ambulance service.

Another woman also witnessed the explosion from her kitchen window. She was Jane McPherson, who lived with her husband John, who was the fire chief in the small town of Fort Lupton. Jane called him from the adjoining room where he had been watching TV, and they stared in disbelief as showers of sparks littered the night sky, lasting fully five minutes, reminiscent of a firework display. Fort Lupton was too far from the scene of the explosion for any loud bang to be heard, though there had been what Jane later described as 'a sort of dull thud'. John McPherson was in a unique position to call assistance, since he had a direct line from his home to the fire station.

Another eyewitness saw and heard the explosion much nearer at hand. The tail assembly of the stricken plane landed on the property of one Conrad Hoppé. His son Kenneth was visiting him at the time, and on hearing a dull roar followed by a mighty blast Kenneth ran out of the house to investigate. There in the sky above his father's farm a plane nose-dived to earth, burning fiercely and leaving a fiery trail of brilliant sparks in its wake. Seconds later there was another explosion and a huge plume of black smoke, shot through with crimson and orange flame, belched up into the sky. Kenneth and his father ran out across the fields to take a closer look. By some fluke, the plane's tail assembly had landed almost intact. The two men could see clearly by the light of the fire the lettering on the side, *United Airlines,* and the number DC 6B, followed by the word *Mainliner.*

Howard Heil, a neighbouring smallholder, joined Conrad Hoppé and his son and the three of them combed the area for survivors as soon as the burning wreckage had cooled sufficiently in the November night air, which did not take very long as the temperature was only two degrees above freezing. They found the bodies of two men who had been thrown clear of the plane. Although unburned, the bodies had hit the earth with such an impact that they had gouged craters a foot deep in the soil. Others had been less fortunate – instead of instant death on impact, they had sustained horrendous burns, most probably while still alive. Unrecognizable charred bodies lay here and there among luggage, torn plane seats, twisted metal and other miscellaneous objects which lay strewn over a wide area. Incongruously, a first-aid kit lay among them, blown open by the blast and spilling its contents among the wreckage. But of survivors there was no sign.

The plane had crashed at a point east of Longmont. Police, fire crews and ambulancemen were soon at the scene, along with dozens of volunteers from neighbouring farms and homesteads. Salvage squads cleared the débris to allow the crews of thirty ambulances to drive in closer to the stricken airliner. Doctors, paramedics, firemen, police and volunteer civilians mingled under the glow of portable arc lights, working from generators which had been set up. The scene in the eerie light was grim.

By the following morning a deep frost rimed the scene as the weary rescuers who had toiled ceaselessly through the night prepared to turn in their reports and go home. They had accounted for everyone on board – a total of thirty-nine passengers and five crew. All forty-four had perished – all forty-four bodies had been found. No survivors had lived to relate their experiences.

The time had now come for the civil aviation authorities to assess the situation and try to ascertain the cause of the crash. Flying conditions had been ideal on the evening of Tuesday, 1 November 1955, when the DC 6B took off, bound for Portland, Oregon. The temperature at take-off was thirty-four degrees; visibility was fifteen miles, and the few clouds that could be seen were drifting very high. Although near-freezing, there was no snow forecast. A team of mechanics had performed the usual routine safety checks before take-off, and ensured that there were no obstructions on the runway. Flight 629 was ready to go.

As the announcement of the flight boomed over the tannoy in the lounge area of Denver's Stapleton Municipal Airport, the passengers gathered up their hand luggage and prepared to board. Most had originally boarded in New York or, later, in Chicago, but four new passengers, all women, had joined the flight at Denver, and at 6.52 p.m. precisely the DC 6B, with Captain Lee Hall at the helm, started on its journey.

Eleven minutes later, Captain Hall radioed back to airport control that the take-off had been successful and that the aircraft was climbing. His report was duly logged in at 7.03 p.m. He gave his position as thirty-five miles out of Denver. Airplanes normally climbed to about 5,000 feet before approaching the foothills of the Rockies, and although Captain Hall had said he was climbing, for some reason he did not state his altitude at the time of his report.

One of the eye-witnesses who had seen the crash from his farm about a mile and a half away was later to state that the plane had been no more than 1,500 feet up at the time, two minutes after the captain had radioed in his report.

Fred B. Lee, administrator of the Civil Aviation Authority, flew at once from its headquarters in Washington, DC, with W.H. Weeks, the chief of the aircraft engineering division, and Ward Masden, the head of the carrier safety division. In Denver, they held an initial conference with representatives of United Airlines, the Airline Pilots' Association, the Flight Engineers' Union, and the company who had manufactured the DC

6B. Special Agent W. Burke of the FBI also participated in the talks. Two other G-men were already working at the scene of the crash, engaged in the grim task of checking the fingerprints of the victims. Another FBI officer, J. William Magee, from the Bureau's forensic laboratory, was studying the twisted wreckage.

As investigators went about the task of questioning witnesses, they noted one common factor in all the eyewitnesses' statements: in every case they had heard *two* explosions: one while the plane was still airborne, and a second when it plummeted to earth. This proved that an in-flight blast had occurred. What they now had to discover was whether the blast had been accidental, or whether it had been caused by deliberate sabotage – in other words, a bomb. In airplane crashes of this kind, rumour is always quick to rear its ugly head, and speculation was rife that terrorists had hijacked the plane and an explosive device had been detonated. Every possibility had to be checked out, despite the fact that it seemed rather unlikely that terrorists would be interested in hijacking an internal flight involving a comparatively small airliner.

A methodical and meticulous search of the wreckage was plotted on a grid map which showed every piece of the shattered aircraft – wreckage had been spread over a two-square-mile area. More than sixty experts worked with the official investigators, each a specialist in his own field. The pattern that emerged showed that the explosion had originated in one of the cargo holds.

Meanwhile, the FBI were investigating the backgrounds of the forty-four victims, their relatives and friends, but they were keeping a low profile. There was as yet no proof that terrorists were involved and the G-men did not want to panic the public unnecessarily. They were not, however, taking any chances.

Buy a methodical process of elimination, technicians were able to delete, one by one, such possible causes as engine trouble, metal fatigue, propeller defects, structural flaws, pilot error, over-heating of pipelines in the fuel system, and so on. There had been no indication of anything wrong radioed in by Captain Hall – the message

he had recorded at 7.03 p.m. had been his last. This in
itself pointed to a sudden catastrophe, of which he had
had no warning. They did find, however, increasing
evidence which would tend to confirm the theory of an
explosion. Pieces of metal were found which did not
appear to have formed part of the aircraft's structure and,
moreover, an odour of gunpowder clung to some of these
pieces. By a series of highly technical tests, they were
eventually able to pinpoint the source of the blast as
having originated in Cargo Hold No. 4. By this time,
investigators felt that the cause of the explosion had been
a bomb planted in a piece of luggage which had been
stowed in that hold. Accordingly, they called in the FBI in
an official capacity to take charge of the investigation, and
accordingly, on Tuesday, 8 November, Roy K. Moore was
appointed in this capacity.

A conference was called which was attended by all the
investigators who could in any way contribute their
knowledge to the probe. 'Let's look at the possibilities,'
Moore said.

We now know it was a bomb and that it was planted in a
suitcase or other piece of luggage stowed in No. 4 hold.
What we do not know is whether it was put on the plane at
New York, Chicago or Denver. Usually these devices,
timed to go off by detonators, do not operate over long
periods of time. We can therefore safely asume that it was
not put on the plane in New York. By the same token, it is
unlikely that it would have been put on in Chicago. I am
firmly convinced, therefore, that in line with other known
short-term timing devices, this bomb was planted in
Denver.

FBI Special Agent Burke now raised a question. 'What is
the usual length of operation of these delayed-action
timing devices?' he said.

'Half an hour is about average, give or take a few
minutes either way,' Moore replied.

'The plane was delayed for a few minutes before
take-off,' an investigator put in. 'That would account for

the device having gone off at the time it did – eleven minutes after the plane had become airborne.'

'What is your opinion on the possibility of a terrorist connection?' another speaker queried.

'Frankly, I don't think so'. Moore looked at the men around him. 'I think it's a mass murderer – a psychotic. Seems to be quite a fashion for them these days. This way, he could kill forty-four at one go instead of individually.'

Burke looked visibly shaken. 'Are you saying that we have a psychopathic mass-murderer right here – in *Denver?*'

'Yes, that's what I figure,' Moore said. 'I don't like the idea any more than you do. In fact I don't like the idea of a mass-murderer anywhere in the country. But all the evidence points to the bomb having been put on the plane in Denver.'

Another participant in the conference asked Moore if he had any other additional evidence that would tend to pinpoint Denver as the airport where the bomb was planted. 'Actually we do,' Moore replied. 'Only four additional passengers joined the plane at Denver. These were all women, and all their luggage was stowed in No. 4 hold. Other luggage was also in that particular hold which had been put on in New York and Chicago but, as we have seen, it is very unlikely that these items contained the bomb. Of course at this stage we do not know if the women, or one of them, was aware of the existence of the bomb, or if one of these women had been used as a dupe by the bomber having, for instance, asked her to take a piece of luggage containing the explosive device on the flight on his behalf.'

Burke deliberated for a moment. Then he looked up. 'Our best bet, it would seem,' he said, 'would be to look for a guy who is either related to, or friendly with, one or more of these four women, and then check into his background for mental instability or a criminal record or both.'

Although Moore was strongly in favour of the Denver theory, he could not allow himself to discount other possibilities. For example, in October there had been industrial action in which feelings had run high. The

Flight Engineers' Union had called a strike, as a result of which the regular flight engineer aboard United Airlines' Flight 629 had been replaced by a substitute, S.F. Arthur. Very few people, however, deemed it feasible that such a labour dispute could possibly be behind the horrific massacre of forty-four persons. In fact, the Union, expressing its horror at the fiendish plot, had already offered a reward of one thousand dollars for information leading to the apprehension of the saboteur.

Every member of the crew, including the substitute flight engineer S.F. Arthur, had friends and in some cases relatives in Denver, and could conceivably have been the target of the bomber. So the FBI set about the task of investigating the backgrounds of all the crew members to see whether there was any evidence of someone bearing a grudge against one of them. Even Captain Hall, First Officer D.A. White, and the stewardesses, Peggy Pettifer and Jacqueline Hinds, were not spared. No leads were forthcoming from these sources.

The FBI had by this time begun seriously to doubt that the atrocity had been perpetrated by a mass-murderer motivated by psychopathic aberrations. Instead, they were beginning to come round to the view that monetary gain might lie behind the outrage. Although this particular kind of crime had never before occured in America, there were cases of the kind that had occurred in Canada, the Philippines and other countries, in which a person had insured the life of a passenger and arranged for an explosive device to be smuggled on board. Moore decided to pursue this angle and see what he could come up with.

Investigations revealed that seventeen of the thirty-nine passengers had purchased flight insurance. This seemed about average, as usually about half of airline passengers insure their flight, while the other half do not bother. Only six of the seventeen had taken out insurance for the maximum amount of cover possible – $62,500. In every case the seventeen policies had been purchased at the airport where the passenger had commenced his or her journey. First Moore was able to eliminate the twenty-two who had not purchased any insurance, and of the seventeen who were insured, all but four had taken out their policies in New York or Chicago. That left just the four women who had boarded at Denver.

Of these four women, two had purchased insurance, in both cases from the Teletrip machine maintained at the airport by the Mutual Insurance Company of Omaha. Katherine Marlow had taken out the maximum insurance of $62,000 by dropping $2.50 in quarters into the machine. Daisy King had paid $1.60 for a policy insuring her for $37,500. Mrs Marlow lived in Washington State and had come to Denver to attend a church meeting. Mrs King lived in Denver. While FBI agents in Seattle checked on the Washington passenger, Moore personally investigated Mrs King.

Mrs King was a widow. She had lived with her son, John Gilbert Graham, aged 23, his 22-year-old wife Marion and their two small children. John was Mrs King's son by her first marriage. John's father died when the boy was three years old. Daisy Graham placed him in a children's home and went out to work as a waitress. Then, in 1940, she had met a wealthy rancher, Earl King. They married soon afterwards and John came home to live with his mother and stepfather.

When John was 15, his stepfather died. John then left home and took various jobs on logging sites and as a construction worker on building sites in Alaska as well as in his native Colorado. Latterly he had taken a night-shift job, with a car hire and rental company in Denver. At the time of the plane crash Mrs King was on the first leg of a journey to Alaska to visit her daughter, John's half-sister. With his background of logging and construction jobs, Moore thought it more than likely that John would have a good working knowledge of explosives. Accordingly the young man was brought in for questioning.

Moore came straight to the point. 'John,' he said, 'the airport records show that your mother's luggage was thirty-seven pounds in excess of the weight limit. She had to pay a surcharge. Do you know why her luggage was so heavy? What was she carrying?'

'I don't know,' Graham replied. 'She did not say anything to me about it.'

'Did you put anything in her luggage?' Moore persisted.

'Your wife did mention something about a Christmas gift.'

'Oh, that!' Graham replied. 'When my mother wasn't looking, I put it into one of her bags as a surprise present. It was only a little thing, though – it certainly did not weigh thirty-seven pounds!'

'What was it?'

'Just a little seashell craft kit. She liked to work with seashells. You stick them on the lids of fancy boxes and stuff like that.'

'Where did you purchase the kit?'

'In a Denver shop, but I can't remember exactly where. I don't remember the name of the shop, or even the name of the street.'

When aides carrying out Moore's instructions combed Denver for two days seeking a shop which stocked such a seashell craft kit, they were unable to find a single store in the whole of Denver or its suburbs that sold such an item.

John Graham was allowed to go, but G-men kept a discreet surveillance on his movements, and also conducted an investigation into his background, which showed that he had a criminal record for petty theft, forging cheques and, what was more ominous, he was suspected of having caused an explosion at the restaurant where his mother worked, although this could not be proved. On 5 September that same year, an explosion wrecked part of the restaurant, and investigators traced the cause to gas escaping from a fuel pipeline which it was found had been deliberately disconnected. The pipeline was ignited by a pilot light on a hot water tank. Graham had told the investigating officers that he had locked up at midnight after assisting his mother, who was in charge of the restaurant while the owner was on holiday. He said that a small amount of money was missing from the cash register. The police, in the absence of any further evidence, had to accept the explanation that a thief had been responsible, though they were at pains to point out that it was, to say the least, highly-unusual that a petty thief would set an explosion in the burgled premises. Graham was not suspected of having any part in it – until now ...

Moore discovered that Mrs King's estate was worth at

least $150,000, inherited from Earl King, and that John Graham was entitled to a half share on the death of his mother. Moore now focused his attention on the insurance that Daisy King had taken out for her trip. Anyone could feed coins into the insurance dispensing machine and fill in a form provided, but this had to be signed by the person taking out the insurance. No such signature was to be found on the form in this case. Two things became apparent: John Graham had taken out the insurance but had been unaware that the signature of the person whose life was being insured was required; it was equally obvious that Mrs King herself had not taken out the insurance, for she would have known that her signature was necessary. It was clear that Mrs King had in fact been totally unaware that John had insured her life for the trip – or at least attempted to. Owing to the absence of his mother's signature he would have stood to benefit not one cent from his ill-conceived plot.

On the afternoon of Sunday, 13 November, John Graham was picked up and brought in for further questioning by FBI agent Roy Moore. He was subjected to an intensive grilling until late the same night. Early the following morning it was announced that Graham had signed a statement, in which he admitted having placed an explosive device in his mother's luggage shortly before she boarded the plane, the intention being to kill her so that he could collect the insurance.

According to the FBI, Graham told them that he had made the bomb about two weeks before the plane crash, using twenty-five sticks of dynamite, a time-clock device with a maximum operational period of ninety minutes, a 6-volt dry cell battery and two dynamite caps, each cap being connected to eight feet of wire, in case one of them should fail. He then concealed the home-made bomb in the trunk of his car. At five o'clock in the afternoon of 1 November he removed the bomb, set the timing device for ninety minutes, and slipped it into one of his mother's luggage bags which were in his mother's car, in which he would be driving her to the airport together with his wife and young son so that they could all see her off.

In order to make room for the bomb, he had to remove

some few miscellaneous items from the luggage bag. These were subsequently found dumped in various garbage bins in the area.

After arriving at Stapleton Municipal Airport terminal, his statement continued, Graham parked the car and carried his mother's three bags to the check-in point. He watched his mother checking in her luggage, after which the family went to the passengers' gate where Graham, his wife and the child said goodbye to his mother and watched her board the plane. There was a delay of a few minutes before the aircraft took off.

Graham, his wife and child went into the airport lounge and ordered coffee. They sat in the lounge for about an hour, and as they were leaving Graham heard one of the cashiers tell another employee that she had heard there had been a plane crash 'about forty miles out of Denver,' although she did not specify which flight it had been. On their return home, later that evening they heard a radio broadcast news bulletin, in which it was reported that Flight 629 from Denver had crashed, killing everyone on board.

Shortly after his confession was announced, Graham was arraigned before US Commissioner Harold S. Oakes, and he was taken to the Denver city jail in handcuffs. His trial opened on 16 April 1956 before Judge Joseph McDonald. Although indicted for each of the forty-four deaths, Graham was tried specifically on the charge of murdering his mother.

For ten days a long procession of prosecution witnesses gave evidence, but when it came to the defence's turn, only three hours were taken up by the witnesses produced by their side. On 4 May the jury retired to consider their verdict, and after only eight minutes' deliberation they returned a unanimous finding of guilty. The judge then pronounced the sentence – Graham was to die in the gas chamber.

In his cell on death row, John Graham signed a document which read in part: 'I accept the verdict of the jury, and desire that it be carried out with all convenient speed. This is my wish.' But at no time was he ever heard to express remorse or regret, for the death of his mother or for the forty-three others – men, women and one small child – who died at his hands.

Graham's scheduled execution date of 30 August 1956 was postponed in order that his counsel might prepare an appeal for clemency. But there was to be no mercy for the man who had shown no clemency to others. Graham displayed the same cool indifference he had shown during his trial when he learned that his appeal had failed, and on 11 January 1957 he was taken to the Colorado State Prison in Canon City. There in the gas chamber one of the most callous murderers in American criminal history met his Maker.

7

Murder at the Post Office

Patrick Henry Sherrill (1986)

Edmond, Oklahoma, is not a very large town, as towns go
– it is a quiet and unassuming community of 50,000,
situated about eighteen miles from Oklahoma City. Crime
is, of course, not unknown there, but it tends to be
confined to the usual petty thefts, taking cars and the odd
domestic fracas. There had been no murders there in
living memory. It was therefore with a sense of disbelief
that a call came in to the police station at 7.30 a.m. on
Wednesday, 20 August 1986, that a gunman was on the
rampage at the post office.

Within minutes of the call being logged by the
dispatcher, a team of armed police, wearing bullet-proof
vests and other protective clothing, was at the scene. As
they arrived, they were greeted by a ominous silence.
There were no signs of activity outside, so it was assumed
that the gunman was still in the building.

With the continued silence, some of the police officers
were beginning to think that this call might have been a
hoax. They conferred as to what the best line of action
would be, and it was decided to telephone the postmaster
who would by this time be in his office. Even if he were
out, one or other of the post office staff would answer the
call. They would thus be able to ascertain exactly what – if
anything – was happening. The call was put through, but
remained unanswered; the telephone could be heard

ringing inside the building.

The police took this as a bad sign, since *someone* would have been in the building: sorters, mailmen, clerks – even if the postmaster had not yet arrived, though he was known to keep the same early working hours as he expected his employees to do. The consensus of opinion at this point was that there was indeed a gunman in the building and that he was holding the staff hostage – which was why no one answered the call.

By 8.15 a.m., with no communication from the staff despite repeated attempts to contact them, and no sound of gunshots being audible from within the building, it was decided to storm the post office. Officers were deployed at various strategic positions around the building, while one detachment shot off the locks to the entrance doors. As they charged in, two shots rang out, followed by silence.

Anyone who had entertained the notion that the call had been a hoax was quickly disabused of such an idea. Officers had literally to step over the bodies of the dead as they entered the building. As the police swarmed all over the post office, survivors, shocked and dazed, who had managed to escape through rear and side exit doors gradually came out of their hiding-places once they realized that it was safe to do so. Only then was the full horror revealed – the horror of a massacre that had taken only ten minutes and left fourteen dead and others wounded.

At just after seven o'clock that morning, a postman, 44-year-old Patrick Henry Sherrill, entered the post office as usual through the staff entrance. He was wearing his uniform and carrying his mailbag slung over his shoulder. He was seen by several other workers, but what they did not know was that his mailbag contained two .45 automatic pistols, a .22 pistol and several dozen rounds of live ammunition. Sherrill uttered not a word but went straight to the sorting room. Delving into the bag, he extracted the two .44s and started firing at random around the sorting office. Richard Esser, 38, of Bethany, Oklahoma, and Michael Rockne, 33, of Edmond, were the first to die. Other sorting room clerks began to flee in panic, screaming to workers in other parts of the building to run for cover.

Sherrill's next target was a group of five women sorting

officers, huddled together under a table. Patricia Gabbard, 47, of Oklahoma City, took the first bullet. Next to die at the hands of the madman was Patricia Chambers, 41, of Wellston, a nearby suburb. The third member of the group to fall victim was Judith Denny, 39, of Edmond. Joanna Hamilton, 30, of Moore, was next, and finally Paula Welch, 27, of Oklahoma City.

Sherrill looked round. The sorting office was not empty – four more co-workers were desperately but vainly attempting to hide beneath or behind the furniture. Thomas Shader, 31, of Bethany, took the first slug, followed by Patty Husband, 49, and Betty Jared, 34, both of Oklahoma City. A fourth worker was critically wounded, but escaped with his life by shamming dead.

The crazed gunman found that he had accounted for everyone in the sorting office, so he next turned his attention to the area outside that room. Kenneth Morey, 49, of Guthrie, walked into this area carrying a bundle of newspapers, apparently having just arrived and unaware of the siege. He was shot dead at point-blank range. While Sherrill was occupied with this victim, three other workers took advantage of his preoccupation with Morey and rushed past him to lock themselves in a vault.

William Miller, 30, of Piedmont, made a valiant but doomed attempt to get out of the line of fire by dropping to the floor and crawling under a table. The berserk executioner spotted the movement and shot him dead.

Sherrill then made his way to the staff canteen, where he saw Lee Phillips, 42, of Choctaw, pouring himself a cup of coffee and helping himself from a box of doughnuts. That was the last meal the unfortunate Phillips was ever to take.

While the gunman was in the canteen, other workers made a dash for the exits to freedom. Their freedom, however, was destined to be short-lived as Sherrill emerged from the canteen and followed them out to the car park behind the building. Jerry Pyle, 51, was dropped in his tracks – the fourteenth person to die at the hands of the madman. Other workers had run out of range of the deadly .44s. Sherrill returned from the car park and re-entered the post office building. It was still only 7.15 –

the carnage had all taken place within a time frame of ten minutes.

Sherrill went into the superintendent's office, where he remained until the police stormed the building at 8.30, when he shot himself dead.

Eyewitness accounts were taken from the postal workers who had managed to escape, either wounded or without physical injury. All were shocked to the core. Police had a hard time trying to obtain coherent statements from the witnesses who, quite understandably, were agitated, even hysterical, sobbing and moaning. One man, Ronald Nagle, who had trained Sherrill in his duties, told police: 'I jumped over the counter and ran like hell. I made it to the exit. All I could think of was getting out of there. But there were many who never made it. The guy was too quick for them.'

Another man described how he lay on the floor, surrounded by bodies, pretending to be dead. 'I wouldn't have survived otherwise,' he told police. 'But for the life of me I couldn't understand what could have made Pat [Sherrill] behave like that. He was clean berserk. There was no stopping him. I used to try to be nice to him, because he didn't seem to have any friends. He was a bit of a weirdo.'

Another co-worker told how he saw a man rush past him bleeding from a bullet hole in his back. 'Pat just suddenly started shooting people,' the man said. 'He shot the supervisor at point-blank range. Then he shot my best friend. After that he just turned around and started spraying the room.' The witness continued: 'I didn't know him very well. He was a bit of a loner. As I understand it, he was clumsy and awkward at his job and didn't seem to know how to carry the mail properly. He got a chewing out from the supervisor yesterday.'

A postman named Robert Logan said: 'Someone yelled out, "He's got a gun!" There was pandemonium. The gunman was just pointing and shooting whoever got in his way. A few of us managed to escape to safety in time, but only a few. It was horrendous. There was blood everywhere.'

One of the three women who managed to lock

themselves in the vault was Marietta Kearns, 33, of Oklahoma City. She told police how she could hear shots, women screaming, men shouting, and the moans of the dying. 'I'll never forget it as long as I live,' she sobbed. 'I stayed there where I was until I heard police arrive, but before that I heard the gunman come right up to the vault door and try the lock. I could hear his heavy breathing. I was really surprised to realize that it was Pat Sherrill – he had seemed such a quiet type.'

As the dead and wounded were transported to hospitals in the area, the Revd Richard Huggins, of the Emmanuel Southern Baptist Church, walked among the bereaved who had gathered outside the post office when they heard the news of the shootings. Many drove miles to ascertain whether relatives employed at the post office had survived, or whether they had been victims of the massacre. While for some there was a joyful reunion, for others there was only the trauma and stress of loss. The clergyman later admitted that his experiences among these people had been traumatic and stressful for him, too, although in a different way.

After Sherrill's body had been removed to the morgue, questions were being asked and theories advanced as to what had triggered his lethal outburst of rage. It was known that Sherrill had received several recent warnings about poor performance from his supervisor, and as a consequence was in fear of losing his job. He had worked at the post office in Edmond for about eighteen months. A spokesman for the postal workers' union said that Sherrill had been reprimanded for sloppy and incorrect methods of mail handling only the day before the shootings, and stated that on previous occasions he had been told he would be sacked if his work standards did not improve.

A neighbour who knew the killer said: 'Pat Sherrill was a real fruit and nut case. He was always angry at something or somebody. Sometimes it seemed he didn't really know himself what he was angry about.'

A check into Sherrill's background revealed that since the death of his mother some years previously he had been practically a recluse. Before that he had served a two-year stint in the US Marine Corps, returning to civilian life in 1966. From that point onwards his mental equilibrium seemed to deteriorate, and he became distinctly eccentric in many of his actions, which led to his being frequently ridiculed. He wore Army fatigues at all times, even to go to church. A neighbour said:

> At first he'd play football with us kids, but after a time he became more of a loner and didn't want to join in our games any more. Some of the other kids called him nicknames, and he didn't like that. He was also suspected of being a Peeping Tom. He carried a pair of binoculars and used to prowl about at all hours of the night. He'd even climb into people's gardens and walk across their lawns.

An Edmond resident who had known Sherrill for fifteen years told investigators that he had never been known to have a girlfriend or any steady relationship. In fact he had never been seen in the company of a woman except his solicitor who dealt with the legal matters arising out of his mother's estate. She says:

> He used to visit me in my office after I had completed all the paperwork in connection with the estate. He never asked me for a date or wanted to form any kind of relationship – he just wanted to keep in touch and talk. He always said that he just happened to be passing my office and would drop in for a chat. I got the impression that he was very lonely and had no friends or anyone to talk to.

Sherrill developed a veritable passion for guns while serving in the US Marine Corps. After his discharge, he joined the Oklahoma National Guard, where he quickly qualified as an expert marksman. He was eventually appointed a weapons instructor, a position he continued to hold until July 1986. It was from the Oklahoma National Guard that he requisitioned the three guns which took the lives of his fourteen innocent victims on 20 August of that year. The unit's armoury superintendent had no idea when he handed Sherrill the guns that they would be used to perpetrate the bloody massacre at Edmond Post Office.

Patrick Sherrill had been due to take part in a national marksmanship trophy competition held in Little Rock,

Arkansas, on 31 August. The Adjutant-General of the Oklahoma National Guard, Maj.-Gen. Robert Morgan, stated: 'There had been no report of any kind, either medical or professional, that would have precluded him [Patrick Sherrill] from serving in the National Guard or from being a member of the National Guard-sponsored marksmanship team selected for the trophy competition.'

According to the Adjutant-General, Sherrill was issued with 200 rounds of .45 calibre ammunition on the Saturday preceding the massacre, to be used in a National Rifle Association-sponsored competition to be held in Arcadia, near Edmond. On the following day, Sunday, he was issued with a further 300 rounds, to be used in the forthcoming competition at Little Rock.

Maj.-Gen. Morgan continued: 'The entire membership of the National Guard of Oklahoma State, with some 12,000 members, deeply regret this incident. They also wish to express their sympathy to the families of the victims.'

While Sherrill's eccentric behaviour had been noted by neighbours and friends, workmates and employers alike, his conduct while on National Guard duties had been exemplary to the very end. No one in that organization could fault him in the smallest detail.

The military life seemed to be the only activity that had given Sherrill a sense of self-respect and self-worth. After leaving the US Marine Corps, he had concocted a story that he had served in Vietnam; this was, however, complete fiction – an ego-boosting fantasy. Official Army records prove that all his soldiering took place in the United States.

When police searched Sherrill's home, they found a daunting arsenal of weaponry. This included a silencer, two air pistols, an air rifle, 3,000 rounds of ammunition, 180 paramilitary magazines, a number of military maps, three sets of Army fatigues, a helmet and a gas mask. There was also a home computer and a video with a large stock of war films on videotape. A curious feature, police observed, wsa that there was only one chair in the entire house; there was nothing for a visitor to sit on. Even the bed folded up into the wall. The one chair was situated in front of the computer desk.

Was there a spark of humanity in the deranged mind of

Patrick Sherrill? According to one co-worker, there was. Madge Larcombe, a 21-year-old postal clerk from Edmond, said that on the day before the killings she had changed from the night shift to the day shift, and Sherrill, it would appear, had tried to ensure that she would not be in the post office at the time he would choose to kill his fourteen victims.

Miss Larcombe's statement read, in part:

> I considered Pat to be a real nutter, but I tried to be nice to him, although it was a bit difficult as he was taciturn and surly. On that Tuesday [the day before the shooting] he questioned me closely about my new work schedule. He wanted to know the hours I would be working on my new shift. He particularly wanted to know that I would not be coming in before eleven o'clock. I thought all these questions were a bit odd, but thought nothing of it as I knew what an oddball he was.

A week before the shootings, Sherrill had confided to her his run-in with the supervisor and how the latter had given him a warning about his work. He had told her that the supervisor was 'always picking on him,' adding, 'One of these days they will be sorry. Mark my words – they'll all be sorry!' Miss Larcombe attached little significance to his words, dismissing them as the fantasy ravings of a 'nutter'.

From the foregoing, it might be construed that Sherrill's mass execution of post office workers was premeditated, hence his solicitousness for a co-worker he obviously liked, and his words about 'everyone being sorry'.

This young woman, too, is a victim, on account of the stress and emotional turmoil she suffered from the knowledge that her co-worker who replaced her on the night shift was one of the women who was shot dead in the crazed gunman's rampage.

The Edmond Post Office, after recovering from the impact of the initial shock, reopened a few days later and carried on its normal services to the public, appointing new staff to take over the duties of those who had died. The townsfolk of Edmond marvelled at, though were not surprised by, the resilience of their kin and the community in general. Flowers filled the lobby, and the voices of both staff and customers were subdued. Few visitors to the post office now would realize what had happened less than five years ago, but the sense of underlying tragedy is never far away from those who were part of it.

8

Uncle Fred

Frederick Nodder (1937)

The school bell rang at four o'clock on 5 January 1937 – the signal for the children who attended the Wesleyan School in Guildhall Street, Newark, Nottinghamshire, to go home after the day's lessons. Miss Daisy Hawley's class of 10-year-olds clattered out, slamming desk lids, swinging school satchels and calling to one another on their way out, as children do. One of these children was Mona Lilian Tinsley, one of the seven children of a respectable coalman and his family who lived in a council house at 11 Thoresby Avenue, Newark. Miss Hawley had described Mona as a bright and intelligent child on her last school report, written at the end of the pre-Christmas term; little did she realize, as she did so, that the first week of the new term would be the last time she would ever see her again alive.

It was Tuesday, 5 January – the second day of the spring term. Mona had gone to school as usual, returning home for her midday dinner and back to school again for afternoon lessons, wearing a light blue jumper and skirt, a brown tweed coat and wellingtons, but no hat. Thoresby Avenue was about twenty minutes' walk from the school, and Mona was expected home at about half past four for her tea. When she did not appear, her parents were not unduly concerned as Mrs Tinsley had a number of relatives in the vicinity and Mona could easily have dropped in to see one of them; she had done so before. On these previous occasions, however, she normally came home by about five o'clock or five-thirty; once she had stayed till six o'clock at the house of a relative whose cat had just had a litter of six kittens. But now, when seven o'clock came and there was still no sign of her, her parents began to feel anxious, and went round to all the houses she could possibly have gone to. Nobody had seen her.

It is unfortunate that the immediate neighbours were not told that Mona was missing, because later two of them, who lived next door in one case and next door-but-one in the other, came forward with vital information, but by then it was too late. Soon after nine o'clock Mr Tinsley reported Mona's disappearance to the police.

Under the supervision of Harry Barnes, the Chief Constable of Newark, a search for the missing child was immediately instituted. Throughout the night the hunt continued; derelict properties in the town were searched, the river-bank likewise, and all motor traffic stopped and the drivers questioned. Early the next morning all the principals of local schools in the area were asked by the police to inform their pupils of Mona Tinsley's disappearance and to invite any child who had any knowledge which could be even remotely helpful to communicate with the police, via his or her parents. Almost immediately, an 11-year-old schoolboy, William Henry Plackett, who did not attend the same school as Mona but lived next door to the Tinsleys at 13 Thoresby Avenue, told police investigators that he had seen Mona near the bus depot with a man. The boy's description of the man was somewhat vague, but he said that he was 'middle-aged' and that he thought that he would probably recognize him again.

The police worked unceasingly during Wednesday, 6 January, making various inquiries around Newark and interviewing bus drivers and conductors. Then it was that the second vital piece of information was volunteered by a woman who had been walking in the direction of Guildhall Street. This woman, a Mrs Annie Hird, lived at 15 Thoresby Avenue and knew the Tinsley family well. Between 3.45 and 4 p.m. she had been on her way to collect her own daughter from the Wesleyan School, and as she approached the building she noticed a man standing in a doorway looking directly at the doorway of the Wesleyan School 'as though he was looking for someone to come out'. As she drew nearer, she then recognized the man as the Tinsleys' former lodger, whom she knew quite well, but they did not speak.

Armed with this slender clue, Harry Barnes went to interview the parents of the missing child again. Wilfred Edward Tinsley and his wife, Lilian Ada, proved to be extremely reticent about their erstwhile lodger. When asked in a casual manner whether they had ever had a lodger, Mrs Tinsley immediately replied, 'Oh, it couldn't possibly be him.' After a certain amount of probing, she eventually admitted that about fifteen months earlier a friend of her sister's had stayed with them for a few weeks, and that he had eventually left because he was unable to pay his rent. Somewhat reluctantly, Mrs Tinsley was persuaded to give the Chief Constable the name and address of her sister, a Mrs Edith Grimes, who lived at 9 Neil Road, in Sheffield.

When interviewed, Mrs Grimes averred that neither she nor her husband had seen this man, whose name was Frederick Nodder, for a considerable time, and Mrs Grimes maintained that she did not know his present address – a most strange statement, since it was subsequently discovered that she visited him regularly every week at his home, and had in fact telephoned him only the previous day.

Patient inquiries on the part of the police soon uncovered a few salient facts about Frederick Nodder. He was a 44-year-old married man separated from his wife, a former private in the RAMC during the First World War and subsequently a motor mechanic, but that he had lost his job on account of dishonesty and intemperance. The break-up of his marriage had followed a court order for the payment of maintenance for an illegitimate child of which he was the father. At that time Nodder was living in Sheffield, but he left the town in order to evade his obligations under this paternity order. Soon afterwards he met the Grimes, who eventually introduced him to the

Tinsleys. Owing to his continued unemployment he found it difficult to meet his financial obligations, and consequently he changed his lodgings several times when he found it impossible to pay the rent.

The Tinsleys gave him a room for some weeks, but despite his good relationship with the family the same difficulty beset him once more and even they could not afford to keep him without his being able to pay his way. In June 1936 he left them and went to live at Peacehaven, a semi-detached house in the village of Hayton, three and a half miles from Retford, where he obtained work with a haulage contractor; but once again drink was his undoing, and he lost this job in due course. Smeath Road, the lonely road in which Peacehaven stood, was at that time unlit and un-made up, and there were only three other properties in the road, all newly built.

The police had a second interview with Mrs Grimes, no more productive of information than the first. They then concentrated on inquiries at bus depots and termini, and by late afternoon on 6 January they had traced the bus driver who had been in charge of the 4.45 p.m. bus to Retford, one Charles Edward Neville, who stated that he had noticed a little girl wearing a brown coat but without a hat, who boarded his bus a little way past the Wesleyan School, accompanied by a middle-aged man, who purchased a return ticket for himself but, he noticed, only a single ticket for the child. They both alighted at Grove Street, Retford.

The police now returned to the Grimes' house and, finding Mrs Grimes just as uncooperative as she had been on the two previous occasions, turned their attention to her husband. Upon questioning of a more pressing kind, he admitted that Nodder had called upon him just after Christmas, but denied any knowledge of the man's present whereabouts. During this interview a neighbour who was at the same time being interrogated by another police officer stated that on 27 December he had noticed a lorry parked outside the Grimes' house, and remembered the word 'Retford'. Mrs Grimes, upon further questioning, denied any knowledge of this lorry and maintained that she had never seen any vehicle parked outside the house at any time.

The police now pursued their inquiries in Retford, where they questioned all haulage contractors and garage owners. It was soon established that a man called Nodder lived in Hayton, three and a half miles away, at a house called Peacehaven in Smeath Road, fifty yards from the Chesterfield Canal, which joins the River Idle at a place called Tiln.

A discreet preliminary inquiry at a neighbouring house elicited the fact that on 6 January a Miss Doreen Jessie Jarman, who worked for the owner of the house as a daily maid, had noticed a little girl wearing a blue jumper and skirt standing at the back door of Nodder's house, and wondered who she might be, as she had never before seen any children at her neighbour's house. She had a very good view of the rear of Nodder's house from the back garden where she had gone to empty ashes in the dustbin.

She thought that the child was eight or nine years old (Mona was very small for a 10-year-old) and stated that at the time she could see Nodder working in his garden. Miss Jarman stated categorically that the time was twelve o'clock, as she had just finished her work for the day (she worked part-time from 8 a.m. to noon each day) and was just about to go home. None of counsel's ploys or suggestions at the subsequent trial could shake her as to the time, and thus it was established that Mona Tinsley was still alive at noon on Wednesday, 6 January.

Further police inquiries failed to produce any evidence of the child having been seen later that day, and that evening Chief Constable Barnes himself decided to visit Peacehaven. The house was deserted and in darkness. Barnes deployed an officer at the house while he returned to headquarters and arranged for other officers to accompany him when he returned later. He and three other officers took up various positions along the unlit road, and at about eleven o'clock their lonely vigil in the dark, cold, blustery January night was rewarded as a figure loomed out of the darkness. After identifying himself, Barnes informed Nodder that he was making inquiries into the disappearance of Mona Tinsley from Newark, to which Nodder replied, 'I know nothing about it.' He was then asked to account for his movements on the previous day, during which he reiterated that he had not seen Mona Tinsley, whom he admitted he knew, for more than a year.

The police were convinced that Nodder had taken the child away, as his description fitted that given by the bus driver and other witnesses, but having no further proof at that stage they removed Nodder to Newark in custody on a holding charge of the non-payment of the affiliation order. While Nodder was in custody his house was searched.

The house was found to be indescribably filthy. A large double bed was the only bed in the house; the sheets were filthy, and under one of the pillows two soiled handkerchiefs, a packet of sweets and a tin of Vaseline were found. Paper was found bearing drawings and scribblings in a childish hand, later proved to be Mona's, and a child's fingerprints were found on unwashed crockery left in the kitchen sink. Clothing similar to the outdoor garments worn by the man seen in the bus was found and sent to the forensic laboratory for tests.

Nodder's recently observed gardening activities were suspect, and police dug up the entire garden, but found nothing. If the child was still alive, where was she? If she was dead – and more than one police officer voiced the opinion that she had been murdered – where had her body been hidden? The surrounding countryside contained innumerable remote and desolate areas where a small body could be successfully concealed; Sherwood Forest alone provided a vast area.

The police fully realized the enormity of the task facing them as they started grimly to search the area systematically. A particular object of suspicion was the Chesterfield Canal, which ran within fifty yards of Nodder's house; for weeks the canal was dragged, along a stretch running for five miles, without result. The water in a culvert running below it was pumped out, and the River Idle itself was also dragged despite the floodwaters caused by the appalling weather conditions prevailing that month. Pits and quarries were searched; cesspools opened and emptied. Police officers waded or stood for hours in muddy water or raging torrents as the search for Mona

Tinsley was relentlessly pursued. Ditches, hedgerows and graveyards were examined; even trunks, cases and boxes left in railway station luggage deposits were officially opened and examined. The grim secret remained unsolved.

While all this unremitting activity was proceeding, including the organization of volunteer search parties in which more than 900 persons from Retford took part, Nodder remained in custody, saying nothing. On 7 January an identification parade was held, at which he was picked out by several witnesses who had seen him on Neville's bus with the child, and also by Mrs Hird and by the boy William Plackett, who knew Nodder as 'Uncle Fred' and who stated that Mona Tinsley also called him by that name. Posters were circulated bearing the missing child's photograph and description, and a police message was broadcast on the national radio wavelength. After these measures had been taken, several more people came forward stating that they had seen Mona with a man, either in the street or on the bus. In every case their description of the man tallied with the suspect's appearance.

Faced with this further evidence, Nodder agreed to make a further statement, which he did at 10 p.m. on 8 January. After being cautioned, he stated that he met Mona near her school, and that she asked him how her auntie (Mrs Grimes) was, and Peter (Mrs Grimes's baby boy). He said that he asked her if she would like him to take her to see her auntie and Peter and that she agreed. He realized that he would be taking a risk if he were seen in Sheffield with the affiliation warrant out against him, so he decided to send the child to her aunt's on the bus with a letter to her aunt explaining his actions. He took her on the 6.45 p.m. bus from Retford to Worksop, giving her full instructions how to get to Neil Road, Sheffield, from Worksop, both verbally and in writing. Then, the statement continued, he returned from Worksop by the 8.15 p.m. bus to Retford, arriving at 8.45, after which he called in at two public houses on the way home, walking via Tiln Lane.

It is difficult to believe that any sane person could have

found Nodder's statement convincing, or even probable. From Nodder's house to Worksop was eleven and a half miles, and from Worksop to Sheffield a further 19 miles. To reach Neil Road from the bus terminus in Sheffield would have meant walking a fair distance to catch a tram, which was a two-penny ride to one end of Neil Road, Mrs Grimes's house being at the opposite end. It must be remembered that it was a dark, cold and very windy January night, and it is hardly credible that anyone in his or her right mind would send a little girl of 10 by herself on such a journey. At the subsequent trial Mrs Grimes stated that Mona had not been to visit her in Sheffield for some years, so she would not have remembered the way in any case. As for Nodder's statement that he did not wish to be seen in Sheffield owing to the risk of his being arrested, this scarcely had the ring of truth, since Nodder visited the Grimes family on 27 December in broad daylight.

At 5.45 p.m. on 10 January, Nodder was charged under Section 56 of the Offences against the Person Act with taking away the child from her parents by force or fraud. The prisoner replied that she had gone with him of her own free will. Acting on Nodder's statement, the police located several persons who had traveled on the 6.45 p.m. bus from Worksop to Sheffield, including the driver and conductor. None of these persons had seen any unaccompanied child on the bus, nor a child accompanied by a man.

Nodder appeared before the magistrates and was remanded until Tuesday, 16 February, when he was committed for trial at the Birmingham Assizes. He pleaded not guilty and reserved his defence, applying for legal aid on the grounds of unemployment.

On 8 March 1937 the trial of Frederick Nodder opened in Birmingham, presided over by Mr Justice Swift, and lasted two days. After hearing all the many witnesses, the jury took only 16 minutes to arrive at their unanimous verdict of guilty, and the judge sentenced Nodder to seven years' penal servitude. The judge's last words to the prisoner were pregnant indeed:

Frederick Nodder, you have been most properly convicted by the jury of a dreadful crime. What you did with that little girl, what became of her, only you know. It may be that time will reveal the dreadful secret which you carry in your breast; I cannot tell, but I am determined that, so far as I have part or lot in that dreadful tragedy of the 5th and 6th January, I will keep you in custody.

Nodder appealed promptly against his conviction, but the appeal was dismissed, and Nodder went to prison to serve his sentence. Meanwhile, the search for Mona Tinsley continued unabated.

* * *

On a fine summer afternoon, Sunday, 6 June 1937, exactly five months after Mona's disappearance, the manager of the local gasworks, a Mr Walter Victor Marshall, of Melwood, Station Road, Newark, was enjoying a leisurely boat trip with his family on the River Idle. While rowing downstream, about three quarters of a mile below Bawtry, he noticed an object in the water which, on the boat's approach, proved to be the body of a female child. Mr Marshall at once moored and sent his son to the nearest police station, and PC Sheridan, accompanied by other officers, arrived within a short time and, with the assistance of Mr Marshall, who used an oar to dislodge the body from the mud and weeds, removed it from about two feet of water and laid it on the river bank. After the arrival of Nottinghamshire County Superintendent Burkitt, the body was taken to the Ship Inn at Newington, and Mr Tinsley was communicated with and brought to identify the body, which he immediately confirmed was that of his daughter Mona. The body was fully clothed in the garments she had been wearing at the time of her disappearance, except for the brown tweed coat and one of her wellingtons. Both these items were found the next day in the mud not far from where her body had been found.

The post-mortem, carried out by pathologist Dr James Webster, showed that the child had been strangled with a ligature and was dead before being put into the water. The body was in an advanced state of adipocere formation owing to long immersion in the water – about five months.

Mud adhered to many parts of the body, filling the mouth and other body cavities and between the fingers. Dr Webster was unable to prove any evidence of criminal assault owing to the advanced state of decomposition of the corpse. After the inquest on 20 July, the pathetic tiny body was buried at Newark, following a funeral service at the Methodist church where she had attended Sunday school.

On 29 July Nodder was brought from prison to the police station at Retford, where he was charged by Superintendent Burkitt with 'feloniously, wilfully and with malice aforethought murdering and killing Mona Lilian Tinsley in the County of Nottingham on the 6th January 1937'. Nodder's reply, after being cautioned before the charge was read to him, was merely that he understood the meaning of the charge.

Nodder's second trial, this time for murder, opened on Monday, 22 November 1937, at the Nottingham Assizes. Like the previous trial, it lasted two days, and was held before Mr Justice Macnaghten in the Shire Hall, Nottingham. Mr Justice Swift, who had presided at the previous trial, did not live to hear the result of the second trial, which proved his prediction to have come true ...

The first day of the trial was spent in examining and cross-examining the witnesses, including the dead child's parents, her neighbours, and the various persons who had seen her with the accused in the street or on the bus. The second day was taken up by the prisoner, who was the sole witness for the defence, giving his evidence. He denied that he had lurked outside the Wesleyan School with any ulterior motive, and averred that he first turned round and saw Mona Tinsley when he heard a child's voice hail him with the words 'Hello, Uncle Fred!' He stuck to his story throughout that she had gone willingly with him in the hope of seeing her aunt and baby cousin, and that he had sent her on the bus from Worksop to Sheffield. Regarding his reluctance to go into Sheffield, he was shown in court the warrant out for his arrest for the non-payment of the paternity order, and agreed that it was correct, but the details were never read out in court.

When asked why he had not first gone with Mona to her

parents' home to ask their permission for taking her to see Mrs Grimes, he gave the feeble excuse that there would not have been time and they would have missed the bus. He said that when Mona reached her aunt's home, Mrs Grimes would herself contact the Tinsleys. His excuse for not actually seeing Mona on to the Sheffield-bound bus was that he did not wish to miss his own bus back to Retford. Finally, he reiterated that he had occasioned no bodily harm to the child.

The jury, and everyone else in the courtroom, thought differently. The jury this time took just thirty-nine minutes to reach their unanimous verdict of guilty of murder, and Mr Justice Mcnaghten, placing the black cap on his wig, sentenced him to death. He was hanged on 30 December 1937 at Lincoln Prison, exactly two months after the death of the judge who had sentenced him at his first trial.

Before pronouncing sentence, Mr Justice Macnaghten spoke some memorable words. 'Frederick Nodder,' he said, 'the jury by their verdict have found that you murdered Mona Lilian Tinsley. Justice has slowly but surely overtaken you.'

Time – five months to the day – had indeed revealed the dreadful secret which Nodder had carried in his breast.

9

The Cannibals of Chicago

Robin Gecht, Eddie Spreitzer
and Andy and Thomas Kokoraleis (1982)

On Wednesday, 8 September 1982, Chicago detective Carey Orr was cruising with two colleagues in their police car when they were notified by their headquarters over their radio to proceed to Stone Street, off Lake Shore Drive, to investigate the death of a 'jumper'. A 'jumper' is American police jargon for a suicide who chooses the messy death of jumping from one of the upper floors of a multi-storey building.

As they entered Stone Street, other squad cars and reporters had already arrived at the scene. Piling out of their car, they made their way to where a body lay, grotesquely sprawled in death in a welter of blood, in an alley between two buildings. Carey Orr and his colleagues bent over the corpse, which was that of a woman of about 30 or so. Her underwear was twisted around her ankles and her upper garments, including her brassière, were bunched up around her neck. 'That sure is no jumper,' Orr observed. 'If you're going to commit suicide you don't strip yourself practically naked before you jump.'

It was the subsequent autopsy report that confirmed that the woman had in fact been murdered, after first suffering horrific injuries before death. She had two black eyes, a split lip and lacerations to both cheeks, signifying that she had been punched in the face by a very heavy-handed assailant. There were two deep gashes across the breasts, and two puncture wounds in the abdomen. There was the livid mark of a ligature around her neck, showing that she had been strangled.

The woman's killer was obviously a sexual psychopath. A 4-inch piece of wood had been thrust into her vagina, rupturing the uterus and the adjacent intestinal wall. Two smaller pieces of wood were found in the abdominal cavity. There were contusions on both legs. The victim had also sustained a fractured skull and a subdural haemorrhage. Blood was lost in quantity from many parts of the body; even if she had not been strangled, the pathologist said, she would have bled to death. The soles of her feet were clean, although no shoes could be found in the vicinity; to the detectives, this indicated that she had not been killed where she was found but dumped at that spot. Anyone who had carried her there would inevitably have been covered in blood, which might help the police to find the killer quickly if he had not had time to burn or otherwise destroy his bloody clothes, take a shower and change.

Owing to the media coverage of the horrific crime, the victim was soon identified as Rose Davis, a 30-year-old advertising executive, of Broadview, Illinois. On 7 September she had spent the day at her office before driving to Chicago's nightclub area where she had arranged to meet her friend Cynthia Romandini, an advertising buyer for an up-market Chicago hotel. After talking for a time on business topics over pre-dinner drinks, they decided to walk around a little before deciding where to dine. An old school friend of Cynthia's happened to be passing, and Cynthia invited him to join them. With him was a Swiss businessman acquaintance who was in Chicago for only a few days to attend an engineering exhibition. Rose Davis invited him to join them, too, to make up a foursome for dinner. The men accepted. They decided to dine at a hotel in the neighbourhood.

At eleven o'clock, when they left the hotel restaurant, the neighbourhood, with its nightclubs, was beginning to come to life. The foursome decided to walk around for a while longer, until finally they moved off in the direction of Rose Davis's parked car. Cynthia and her friend waited beside the Volkswagen, expecting that Rose and the Swiss businessman, who had somehow fallen behind and were about a block to the rear of them, would reach the car in a matter of minutes. When half an hour passed and there was no sign of them, Cynthia and her friend assumed that the other couple had made other plans. They left the car, hailed a cab, and shared the ride until Cynthia reached her apartment, after which her friend continued on his way to his own abode.

Detectives soon traced the movements of the two couples, and before long the Swiss businessman had been located and was nervously sweating it out in police custody. Speaking broken English with a heavy German accent, he explained the missing half hour while Cynthia and her friend had waited for them beside Rose Davis's car. He said that he and Rose decided to walk to Oak Street Beach, which was only a few yards away. He then invited Rose back to his hotel room, but she declined, whereupon he walked her back to her car. By that time Cynthia and her companion had already left. Leaving her beside the car, where she said she would wait to see if her friends came back, he then walked off to his hotel a few blocks away.

Interviews with hotel staff verified that the visitor from Switzerland had returned alone to his hotel at the time he said he had, and that nothing about him seemed to be amiss either in his behaviour or dress. He also voluntarily agreed to take a polygraph (lie-detector) test, which he passed easily. Police decided that he could not possibly have been involved in the murder, and he was released.

Within hours of his release he was hot-footing it to the airport to fly back home, all thoughts of the next day of the engineering exhibition forgotten. To become mixed up in a murder scandal would cause a good deal of unwelcome publicity and embarrassment to his company, and might even cost him his job. That visit to Chicago was one he would prefer to forget. He would plead indisposition as an excuse to his superiors for flying home early.

The investigation dragged on for forty-two days after

the murder without any lead to a suspect, but on the forty-second day – 20 October 1982 – an incident occurred which would indirectly lead to a breakthrough in the case – one that none of the investigating officers could possibly have foreseen. A sadistic attack was made on a Chicago prostitute in a red Dodge van. She had entered the van quite willingly, but once inside the doors had been slammed shut and bolted and she had been subjected to a horrific attack with a butcher's knife. Her assailant had also drawn a gun on her and forced her to commit various deviant sexual acts, after which she was handcuffed to a metal upright strut which formed part of the van's internal wall structure. She was then forced at gunpoint to swallow a number of drugs. The last thing she remembered was her captor driving off to an unknown location, before finally losing consciousness. She woke up the following day in the Illinois Masonic Hospital.

It was there that it was discovered what had been done to her. Her left breast had been entirely severed, and her right breast was barely attached to her body. When she had recovered sufficiently from the effects of the anaesthetic after surgery, she was able to give the police a good description of both the red Dodge van and of her attacker, who had left her for dead, dumped in a disused lot. She described her attacker as a white male in his late twenties to early thirties, of slender build, shortish and with wavy sandy hair, who spoke with a faint trace of a Southern drawl. She said that she would know him again if she saw him.

The same day, two Chicago Precinct 5 detectives, Thomas Flynn and Philip Murphy, could scarcely believe their luck when they spotted a red Dodge van answering to the description of the wanted suspect vehicle in every respect: obscured glass side windows, no rear windows, and some kind of mascot in the form of a bulldog clip holding two large feathers, one white and one blue, fastened to the driver's mirror on the outside of the vehicle. Flynn and Murphy cut in and pulled the van over to the kerb.

The driver seemed to be somewhat nervous, but agreed to answer the officers' questions. He gave his name as

Edward Spreitzer, aged 21, and said that the van belonged to his boss, Robin Gecht. The two of them were renovating a basement apartment a few blocks away. The detectives saw that Spreitzer did not fit the description of the suspect described by the hospitalized prostitute, so they asked him to leave the van parked and accompany them in their car to the site where he and Robin Gecht were working. Perhaps Gecht might match the wanted man's description?

The two detectives asked Spreitzer to fetch his boss, as they wished to question him about the van. As they sat in their car outside, Spreitzer returned with Gecht. They observed that he was 5ft. 7in. tall, about 140 pounds, very slender and sandy-haired. When he answered the officers' questions, he spoke with an unmistakable Southern drawl, albeit a faint one. The detectives informed Gecht that they were making inquiries regarding his van and requested him to accompany them to police headquarters. Gecht willingly agreed. At the same time, the detectives said, they would like Spreitzer to come too. The latter told them that they would have to leave two other men working in the apartment. Instead, the officers asked him to fetch them as they would like to talk to them as well. As one of the officers remarked later, 'Never were four suspects rounded up with less hassle.'

Once Gecht, Spreitzer and the two other men were safely at police headquarters, they were quickly separated for interview in four separate rooms.

All four willingly consented to have their photographs taken, but they were not asked to provide fingerprints at this stage. The mugshots, together with several others from police files of similar-looking men, were rushed to the Illinois Masonic Hospital and shown to the mutilated prostitute. She was still in a critical condition, but when shown the photographs she immediately picked out the one of Gecht as the man who had attacked her. 'He's even wearing the same shirt!' she told detectives at her bedside.

Gecht and his three workers were then driven under police guard to the hospital, where a line-up was held, using four hospital workers of similar build and height as additional identity parade volunteers. Owing to the severity of her injuries, the woman was unable to walk and was taken to view the line-up in a wheelchair. So that everyone would be at eye-level, the suspects and their co-paraders were also seated. As soon as she saw Gecht, the victim pointed to him and shrieked 'That's him!'

Gecht and the other three men were returned to police headquarters, where Gecht's shirt, shoes and other garments were taken away for forensic examination. Gecht was charged with rape, aggravated battery, sexual assault, kidnapping and attempted murder. He was held in custody for several days, until a friend posted bail for him, when the police had no choice but to release him, under the provisions of the law. They openly voiced their reluctance to allow him to walk free.

The other three men held with Gecht were also released, since no evidence was forthcoming that they had played any part in the rape, torture and mutilation of the young prostitute who was still in hospital recovering from surgery.

On 25 November a young woman reported to the police that a man had attacked her with an axe. Her description of her attacker exactly fitted Robin Gecht. A warrant was issued for his arrest and he was picked up in Carpentersville, Illinois, where he had moved in order to avoid the publicity which had followed his original arrest. He was unceremoniously bundled into a police car and brought back to Chicago's Area 5 Precinct, where all the same detectives were waiting for him who had interviewed him on the previous occasion. Gecht expressed his willingness to assist the police with their investigation, but denied that he had been involved in committing any crime. His buddy, Eddie Spreitzer, was also picked up for questioning.

Eddie Spreitzer was of a different calibre altogether from Robin Gecht. He began to crumble soon after the experienced detectives set to work breaking down his defences. Soon he was spilling out to horrified detectives details of a series of horrific murders which he, Robin Gecht, and a third man, Andy Kokoraleis, had committed over the preceding eighteen months. All the victims were young women, and one of them was Rose Davis, the woman whose body had been found in the alley between two buildings in Stone Street.

Spreitzer described to the officers how the murder of Rose Davis occurred. He, Gecht and Kokoraleis were cruising the nightclub area, looking for a prospective victim, when they spotted Rose Davis standing beside her parked car. Gecht, who was driving the red Dodge van, called out to her. 'Do you want to come for a ride with us and have some fun?' he said. 'No,' she replied, 'I am waiting for my friends.'

Gecht then gave the prearranged signal – five taps on the van's plywood partition – to his friends, whereupon Spreitzer and Kokoraleis jumped from the vehicle and grabbed Rose Davis, dragging her forcibly into the back of the van. As the woman began screaming in panic, Spreitzer punched her in the face until she stopped. Then, according to Spreitzer's account, Gecht drove to a secluded spot in the vicinity of Lake Shore Drive and stopped the van. He raped the woman and carved and slashed her breasts with a small axe. He then thrust the handle of the weapon into her vagina. By this time Rose Davis was, mercifully, unconscious. Kokoraleis then stabbed her in the abdomen with a knife. The dead woman's body was then dumped in the alley between two buildings where it was later found.

Kokoraleis was picked up by the police and quickly confessed to his part in the saga of murder and mutilation which was unfolding. From 5 to 8 November the three men, who were all interrogated separately, corroborated each other's statements during the three days of questioning. Andy Kokoraleis also implicated his brother Thomas in the grisly catalogue of crimes. Thomas Kokoraleis was picked up by the police and he, like his brother and Spreitzer, soon cracked under interrogation. Only Gecht remained obdurate and refused to admit to any murders, although he admitted being the owner of the red van. Since the vehicle was registered in his name, he could hardly deny this.

Thomas Kokoraleis was the member of this gruesome group who was to provide the police with their greatest shock, when he told the interrogating officers that all four of them had indulged in cannibalism on several occasions. Breasts were cut off their victims' bodies and this was done in at least one case while the victim was still alive, as the hospitalized prostitute was able to testify. These were then carried up to Gecht's attic apartment and used in bizarre and grisly 'ceremonies' in which all four took part. A home-made 'altar', covered with a red cloth, was used, lit by two candles, in a darkened room. Gecht would place the breasts on this structure, and start the 'ceremony' by reading from the Bible. The four men then took turns masturbating into the breast, or sometimes they would perform this action simultaneously. Afterwards the breast would be cut into small portions and eaten raw.

At their trial, Gecht was found guilty of the attack upon and mutilation of the prostitute, for which he received a term totalling 120 years in prison. Eddie Spreitzer confessed to four murders, including that of Rose Davis, and accounting for three other unsolved mutilation murders during the previous year in the state of Illinois. He was sentenced to life in prison. In 1986 a further hitherto unsolved murder was attributed to him, and he was brought from Joliet Penitentiary to face trial for this mutilation killing of a 19-year-old prostitute. His sentence was changed from life imprisonment to death in the electric chair. He was told that he could plea-bargain this decision to be commuted back to life imprisonment if he would agree to testify against Robin Gecht, but he refused.

Andy Kokoraleis was sentenced to life imprisonment without any chance of parole for the murder of Rose Davis, and his brother Thomas was found guilty of the murder of a young secretary in Elmhurst, Illinois, whose body was found, minus breasts, in a disused lot on the outskirts of the town. He, too, will have no chance of parole during his term of life imprisonment.

10
Circumstantial Evidence
Unsolved (1931)

Vera Page lived with her parents in a ground-floor maisonette in Blenheim Crescent, Notting Hill Gate, London. Although tall for a 10-year-old, her elfin features offset the first superficial impression of an older child. She had a ready, winning smile and a trusting nature but, as Mr S. Ingleby Oddie, the Coroner, pointed out at the inquest, these did not save her from meeting a horrible death at the hands of 'a fiend in human form' who brutally outraged and then murdered her.

On Monday, 14 December 1931, Vera returned home from school at the usual time, about 4.30 p.m., for her tea. It was, of course, dark at the time. Her mother told her that tea was not yet ready, as she was baking a cake which she had only just put in the oven. On Vera's remarking to her mother that she was hungry, Mrs Page told her that she would have to wait, and that tea would be ready at half-past five that day. So Vera asked her mother whether she could in the meantime go round to her aunt's, who lived only a short distance away, to show her aunt her swimming certificates, of which she was very proud. Her mother gave her permission.

Vera never returned home for her tea. At first Vera's mother thought she had stayed to have tea with her aunt, but as time passed she began to think she was mistaken in such an assumption. She decided to wait for her husband, who was a painter with the Great Western Railway at Paddington, to return home from work, and then, after telling him, leave the house to make inquiries to see if she could find out where Vera had got to. She, of course, first visited her sister, who informed her that, after showing her the swimming certificates and having a cup of tea and a few biscuits, Vera had left her house at about a quarter to five, saying that she was going straight home. Mrs Page then called on a few neighbours whose children were school-friends of her daughter, but none of them had seen her.

Greatly alarmed by now, Mrs Page informed her husband that no one knew where Vera was, or where she could have gone after leaving her aunt's, and Mr Page immediately went to the police station to report her missing.

The police soon found a person who had seen Vera on her way home from her aunt's, clutching her swimming certificates in a large manilla envelope. This witness, however, stated that Vera had hurried past her home in Blenheim Crescent, the time being about five o'clock – the time when she could have reasonably been expected to arrive home from her aunt's house. A few minutes later another witness, also a neighbour, stated that she saw Vera looking in the brightly lit window of a chemist's shop some little distance past her home, which was full of Christmas decorations and gifts.

All these leads seemed very reasonable – Christmas was approaching, and the child doubtless wished to choose gifts for her family to purchase with her pocket-money; several school friends later interviewed told police that Vera had in fact mentioned several of the gift items she had in mind, and it was confirmed that these were all stocked by the chemist. Bath cubes, fancy soaps – toiletries of that kind were what Vera had in mind for her modest gifts.

However, the police now found two more witnesses who gave very different and disturbing accounts. One said that she had seen Vera still looking in the shop window at 6.30 p.m. – most odd, indeed. Even stranger was the statement of another witness who claimed to have seen Vera walking along Montpelier Street, which was a good quarter of a mile farther on from the chemist's and even farther away from her home. This last witness said that the time was 6.45 p.m., and also mentioned that Vera was swinging her school beret in her hand, but could not remember whether or not the child was carrying a brown manilla envelope. These strange sightings were even more unaccountable in the light of the fact that Vera had expressed a wish for an early tea to her mother, and had told her aunt that she was going straight home as she was hungry.

The following day saw Vera's features staring at millions of readers from the pages of their daily newspapers, and in addition the BBC broadcast a description of the missing child over the radio and asked anyone who thought they had seen her to inform the police.

Twenty-four hours later a milk roundsman, William Smith, was delivering in Addison Road, Notting Hill, at some time between 9 and 9.30 a.m. Many of these houses had evergreen shrubs in their front gardens, some of these forming hedges inside the wooden fences, others grouped together in the gardens to form screens to add to the privacy of the houses. As Smith walked up the garden path to deliver milk to one of these houses, he caught sight of what looked like a bundle of clothing, partly concealed by this screen of shrubbery. Curious, he put the milk bottles down on the path and moved towards the shrubbery to investigate. It was the fully clothed body of Vera Page.

On the arrival of the police the first thing that struck them was the dry condition of the body, despite the damp and dripping vegetation in the garden. It had rained heavily the previous night and the pavements were still wet. This meant that the body had been transported and dumped in the garden only a short time before Smith came on the scene. The police also noted that Vera's school beret was missing, and there was no sign of the envelope containing the swimming certificates.

It was thought that perhaps a costermonger's barrow had been used to transport the body, since it would have aroused no curiosity from passers-by; the darkness of the December morning would also have afforded cover to the person seeking a place of concealment for his dreadful burden. The tradesmen's entrance to the house led directly on to the area of shrubbery where the body was found, so that its depositor would not have had to enter the front gate or cross the garden path.

The pathologist's report confirmed that the child had been dead for about forty-eight hours, and that she had been savagely and forcibly raped and afterwards strangled. Although the body was fully clothed, her knickers had been ripped down the front from top to bottom. Coal dust was found on her face and body and on all her clothes; this suggested that the child had either been killed in a coal cellar, or that she had perhaps been killed elsewhere and her body subsequently hidden in a coal cellar until such time as the killer deemed it safe to venture abroad to dispose of it. Blobs of candle-grease were found on the clothing, which seemed to imply that the coal cellar was devoid of electricity and that the killer had been compelled to carry out his awful purpose by candle-light.

A ligature, possibly rope or cord, had been tightened round the child's neck after death, although she had been killed by manual strangulation. Police thought that such a rope or cord had been used to assist the killer in carrying the body to a place of concealment.

Caught in the bend of the dead child's right elbow was a grimy finger-stall that had apparently slipped off the murderer's finger as he had carried her and dumped her in the garden. This consisted of a length of dirty bandage wound round and round to fit a finger, containing a stained strip of lint, which pathololgists stated had been in contact with a septic finger.

The police had indeed little to go on – few real clues, and only one or two witnesses who could really be said to provide any lead. They were understandably sceptical of the two witnesses who had said they saw Vera at 6.30 and 6.45 p.m., alone and apparently unaccompanied, and seemingly in normal good spirits. They therefore decided on a massive inch-by-inch search of the immediate area, in particular keeping a lookout for the missing red school beret and the brown manilla envelope containing swimming certificates.

Quite soon the police had their first real break – a red school beret, subsequently identified as Vera's, in the basement area of a shabby house in Stanley Crescent. Not far away from the beret lay a discarded candle-stub.

In the basement area was a door which led to a basement flat. The police were soon interviewing the old woman who lived in this flat, who readily gave them permission to search her coal cellar at the opposite end of the area. The door was unlocked, and as the police entered – the tenant stated that the key had been lost long ago – they noticed an old metal candlestick lying on the pile of coal, but nothing else of note. The old woman told them that between 8 and 9 o'clock that evening she had gone to sweep up the area and the beret was certainly not there then. However, she did say that there were several torn-up scraps of white card littering the area, which she had swept up and burnt in the kitchen boiler. Police thought that these might possibly have been the swimming certificates – now gone beyond recall. The woman did not recollect a brown manilla envelope or pieces of such an item.

The police now questioned the tenant as to whether she had heard any strange noises, or the footsteps of any intruder in the area. She stated that she always kept the wireless on at full volume, so as to deter would-be intruders or burglars, so she had not heard anybody.

Superintendent George Cornish, who was leading the Scotland Yard team working on the case, now realized that it was well within the bounds of possibility that the murder could have been committed in the coal cellar of the Stanley Crescent house, or at least the body hidden there for a period of time prior to its deposition in Addison Road. Stanley Crescent was very close to Montpelier Street, where Vera had reportedly been seen walking at 6.45 on the night of her disappearance, though the police were at a loss to explain the anomaly of her having gone to the Montpelier Street area alone, if the witnesses were to be believed.

Minute examination of the coal cellar by forensic scientists failed to establish any proof that a body had been concealed there, much less that a murder had been committed. There were no fingerprints or footprints of any kind, either in the coal dust or on the door or door-handle, or even on the candlestick which had been found among the coal. The red beret, although said to be that worn by Vera Page, was similar to dozens of other berets worn by pupils who attended Vera's school, and it did not contain any name tape or other distinctive marking. The woman tenant of the basement flat told police that she thought the torn-up pieces of white paper might have had lettering on them, but she could not be sure: 'It was just litter to me.' The swimming certificates had been printed on white paper with red lettering, but the memory of a 75-year-old woman and a few ashes in the bottom of the boiler were no proof at all. The Superintendent and his men were still groping in the dark.

Superintendent Cornish decided to interview the sorrowing parents to see whether he could find out anything about the immediate neighbours and their movements – a slender hope, perhaps, but George Cornish was not a man to leave even a small pebble unturned. Mrs Page told him that although Vera was friendly and confiding towards people she knew, she considered it unlikely that she would be so disposed towards strangers, with whom she was shy and diffident. This gave Cornish the idea that the man who had lured Vera to her death might have been someone who was known to her and with whom she would not have been afraid to go. In particular, she would have been completely trusting if such a person were a friend of her parents.

Cornish now asked the Pages for details of any persons who were friendly with them and who knew Vera well enough to be on good speaking terms. They told him of a young man who visited his parents every week in the upper part of the house above the Pages' maisonette. This man, who worked in a local laundry, always had a friendly word for both Mr and Mrs Page and for Vera whenever he visited the house – indeed, he had been invited in to tea by them many times.

The Superintendent was more than interested to be

informed by the Pages that on the last occasion they had seen this man he had a bandage on his left hand, although Mrs Page, who had noticed this, could not remember which finger was bandaged, although she was sure it was a finger, and not a palm or other hand wound.

The bandage that had been found in the crook of the child's arm was of a common type that could be purchased anywhere for a few pence. The material inside was ordinary boric lint – again, a common material in first-aid boxes. As to the laundry worker, he could easily have cut his finger on a machine at work and had it dressed by the first-aid attendant at the works.

Armed only with this slender clue, Cornish decided to interview the laundryman, 41-year-old Percy Orlando Rush, who looked much younger than his age – he could easily be taken for 30. He was shown the grubby bandage and asked to fit it on his hand. Cornish observed that his left little finger had two now healed cuts on it. The finger-stall fitted exactly over this finger. As the laundryman handed it back to the Yard man, his face was expressionless and he showed no signs of agitation or concern.

'Is this the finger-stall you lost?' asked Cornish.

'I certainly did lose one, though I've no idea when or where,' Rush replied. 'The cuts were still bleeding, so I got another. I've still got it somewhere.' Rush rummaged in a drawer and produced another equally grubby finger-stall, folded in exactly the same way as the one in the Yard's possession, and similarly containing a stained piece of boric lint.

'Can you try to remember when and where you lost the first one?' persisted Cornish.

'Sorry mate,' replied Rush. 'No idea.' He looked straight into Cornish's eyes. 'I just got home from work one night and found it had come off. It was still bleeding, so I fixed it up with another one.'

Cornish was a frustrated man. He had a growing conviction that he was wasting his time, but he was not to be deterred in his search for the truth. He seemed to have some pieces of a jigsaw puzzle, none of which fitted together, and all of which were entirely dependent on his finding the other missing pieces. What did he have? A red beret and a candle-stub found near a coal cellar; coal dust on the body; the child's beret not with the body; the swimming certificates missing, and a woman who lived in the same house as the coal cellar saying she had swept up and destroyed some litter which could possibly have been the missing certificates. No prints of any kind in or about the coal cellar. Candle-grease on the child's clothes. A bandage found on the body which could possibly have been worn by the laundry worker and again, it might not. A bandage similar to thousands of other bandages.

It was all too little to go on. Circumstantial evidence at best. And Cornish did not really take the two witnesses too seriously who had said they had seen Vera at 6.30 and 6.45 p.m., despite the proximity of Montpelier Street to Stanley Crescent. No, this was no peg on which to hang a murder. No way would it stick in a court of law.

Cornish next decided to check up on the laudryman's whereabouts on the night of the murder, and in particular the time he had left the laundry, the time he had reached home, and where he had been in the meantime. Rush stated that he left work on the Monday night at his usual time, 5.55 p.m., and that although he usually went straight home he did not do so that night as his wife was going to her mother's and she would not be back until about 8.30 p.m. So he took his time going home, doing some shopping along the way.

Although Rush remembered which shops he had visited, none of the shopkeepers could remember him. In the 1930s most shops remained open until 9 or 10 p.m. and were far too busy serving customers to take much notice of what they looked like. An ordinary-looking average working chap would pass unobserved in a crowd.

Rush told Cornish that he arrived home at about 8.30, to find that his wife had preceded him by about a quarter of an hour and was in fact already cooking their supper. His wife confirmed this story and even remembered that her husband had purchased a packet of wooden clothes pegs, a couple of sausage rolls for his lunch the next day, half a dozen eggs, some cigarettes for both of them, a pound of ground rice and a Harvo malt loaf. If George Cornish had the fleeting impression that these two were a pair with a ready-made story to answer any questions he might ask them, he would have to keep his thoughts to himself …

Cornish could find no flaw in the story provided by the couple, who appeared to have a cast-iron alibi. Only the matter of the finger stall niggled at his consciousness. Although hopeful as a tenuous clue, there was no proof whatsoever that it had been worn by the man he had just interviewed. If he could have caught the man out in an untruth, then perhaps he could have had some chance in tying it in. Without such a loophole, however, there was more – much more – than a reasonable doubt, as a court of law would put it. No judge would possibly have convicted such a defendant.

Rush readily admitted that he knew Vera Page quite well, but stated that he had not seen her on that fateful Monday night, and in fact could not have done so as he did not go out that evening and in any case he did not visit his parents on Mondays. He also volunteered the information that he had only ever seen her in her indoor clothes and would probably not recognize her wearing her outdoor things, especially in the dark: 'These kids all look alike in their school uniforms.'

Cornish felt that the case would remain unsolved on the files, and he was right. He had no case against the laundry worker, who had to be accepted as innocent. This is why the law had no grounds for taking him to court. The fact remained, however, that Vera Page had been raped and murdered in a most brutal fashion. The newspapers carried banner headlines about 'a man helping police with their inquiries', but when no arrest was made the stories ended suddenly. Behind the scenes, however, the police were continuing with their investigations with unremitting thoroughness.

One of the mysteries of the case was the identity of the person who had given Vera a meal shortly before her death. The child had left home hungry, and at her aunt's had received only a cup of tea and three or four biscuits. She had never returned home. But among the coal dust and mud on her clothes when she was found were vomit stains which, when analysed by forensic scientists, proved conclusively that she had eaten a substantial meal shortly before her death, and that the act of strangulation had forced upwards undigested food in the form of vomiting. Who had given Vera her last meal? Had the killer lured the hungry child to her doom by offering her food?

The finger-stall seemed still the most likely line of investigation. Detailed technical consultations were held with cotton experts in Manchester. Technicians examined and compared the fabric of the finger-stall found with the body with that of the finger-stall the laundryman had produced to Cornish when interviewed. The findings of the experts proved that, although these fabrics were similar, they were not identical and could not have been cut from the same roll. Cornish's hopes were thus dashed further. Any chance of pinning even such a slender clue on his hypothetical suspect had by now rapidly receded. In short, the two bandages had been purchased from two different shops carrying similar but not identical stocks, which had come from different suppliers. It was, of course, possible, but rather unlikely, that the suspect, or anyone else for that matter, who had a settled home and place of employment, would purchase bandages to be used continuously from two different shops.

A woman was located who had seen a man pushing a barrow in the direction of Addison Road on the morning that the body was found. An identity parade was set up in which Rush was asked to take part, which he did willingly. The woman picked out the wrong man. A second line-up was arranged, Rush again participating, and again the woman picked out another man. She apologized to the police and explained that it was only just getting light when she had seen the man pushing the barrow. She said she thought that some object in the barrow was covered by what looked like a red tablecloth. A tablecloth of the same colour was found at Rush's home, but more than 400 other households in the immediate vicinity were subsequently found to have similar red tablecloths!

At the inquest the jury was directed by the Coroner, Mr S. Ingleby Oddie, that in the absence of vital links in the chain of circumstantial evidence, the only proper course was to return an open verdict of murder against some person or persons unknown. In conclusion Mr Ingleby Oddie said: 'This is the most interesting and horrible inquest I have ever held, and thus it has been my lot to bring it to so unsatisfactory a conclusion.'

Many police officers on the investigation refused to consider the case closed, although officially it was so designated. They waited for years for some chance to bring to light some factor not hitherto covered by the previous inquiries. But the murderer of Vera Page remained – officially – unknown.

Vera was buried on 23 December 1931. Hundreds of people lined the streets as the funeral cortège made its way slowly to the cemetery, and mingling among the crowds were the police officers who knew that somewhere, someone walked free among them who had snuffed out the life of a 10-year-old child as the price of his perverted lust.

11
A Date with Old Sparky

Robert Long (1984)

Karen Beth Dinsfriend was beautiful by anybody's standards. She was 28 years old, a slender brunette with long, silky hair and hazel eyes. She had a bright future before her, having been raised in a comfortable middle-class home in St Petersburg, Florida. Although she had graduated high school with good grades, she had for some unaccountable reason taken no interest in furthering her career or finding employment appropriate to her undoubted assets of good looks and an above-average IQ. Instead, she drifted into drugs and prostitution. Everyone who had known her said what a terrible waste her life had become. Some offered to help her in various ways, but she was indifferent to the pleas of family and friends.

In 1982 Karen was sent to prison for forging prescriptions to obtain drugs in Tallahassee, the state capital. Released the following year, she returned to St Petersburg and took a job as a hostess in a restaurant. For a few months she managed to keep off the drugs until she met an old friend who supplied her with heroin, and from that point onwards Karen's life was doomed.

On 4 January 1984 Karen Dinsfriend was arrested in St Petersburg for prostitution, and in the pocket of her jacket police found a vial of cocaine. She was sent to a drug rehabilitation centre, but absconded. If only she had decided to make one more last attempt to kick the drug habit, this beautiful young woman's life might have been turned to good account. Instead, her semi-naked body was fished from a lake near Tampa, Florida, on 14 October that same year. Karen Dinsfriend had not committed suicide, nor had she fallen into the water by misadventure. She had been bound with ropes and brutally beaten to death.

Karen Dinsfriend was not the first of Florida's young women to be found murdered that year. On 13 May 1984 the body of a pretty 19-year-old Vietnamese girl was found, bound and gagged, in a field beside Interstate Highway 75, near Tampa, Florida. A post-mortem found that she had been raped and strangled. She was identified as Ngeon Thi Long, known as 'Peggy', who had come to Florida from her family home in California. In Tampa she had found employment as a 'go-go dancer' in one of the nightclubs on Tampa's Nebraska Avenue strip. Unlike some of the other dancers on the Strip, Peggy was not a prostitute, but she was into drugs. The owner of the nightclub where Peggy worked was to say later that she was always trying to get rides from customers because she did not have her own car. 'She was great fun – a bubbly sort of girl,' he said. 'Pity she was into drugs, though, because she said she had an ambition to study fine arts in college one day.'

One night, in the middle of May, about three months after she had started work at the club, she failed to show up. There was no telephone call to say she was sick, and none of her friends at the club had a clue as to what had happened to prevent her from coming in to work. 'It was quite out of character for her,' the club owner said. 'She was always very reliable and would even let me know if she was going to be a few minutes delayed.' Police were asked to see if they could locate her. She had last been seen leaving a club near the campus of the University of South Florida; there the trail ended.

On the afternoon of Sunday, 13 May, her body was found. Police had few clues because Peggy was a comparative newcomer to the area and had fewer friends than someone who had lived in the area for a longer time would have had. The investigation wound down with no leads to the killer of the part-Vietnamese dancer.

Only a few days later police were to realize that a

psychopathic killer was loose in their midst. On 26 May the nude body of a young woman, brutally beaten and bound, raped and strangled, was discovered in a wooded area outside Tampa.

The body was that of Michelle Denise Simms, another emigré to Florida from California. Aged 22, the green-eyed brunette moved in with a couple who had an apartment in Fort Pierce, on Florida's Atlantic coast. The couple were friends from her California days, and had employed Michelle as a despatcher for their trucking company. Soon after they moved to Florida, Michelle also decided to relocate to the Sunshine State. After first obtaining jobs as a receptionist to a dentist and then to a veterinary surgeon, she finally opted for a much more highly-paid job as a masseuse. The massage parlour where she worked firmly discouraged its employees from offering any more personal services to its clients, and Michelle had no wish to become a prostitute. Drugs, however, were to be her undoing.

On Sunday, 29 April, Michelle was stopped as she drove her car along the highway by patrolmen doing spot checks for drivers who were using the highway without benefit of driving licence or insurance, and while the officers found her car documents in order they discovered eight caps of cocaine and half an ounce of marijuana in the glove compartment. Michelle was arrested, taken to court the following day and fined a hundred dollars.

Towards the end of May Michelle left Fort Pierce, accompanied by a girl friend, in her car. She drove from Fort Pierce to Tampa, arriving on Saturday, 26 May. The following day her body was discovered in the copse not far from the city.

Michelle was known to have called her sister a week after her arrest. During this conversation she told her sister of her arrest and also informed her that she was going to leave Fort Pierce and relocate in Tampa. 'Michelle was a lovely girl,' her sister was to say later, 'but she was very confused. She never seemed to know exactly what she wanted. She was restless and always on the move.' The sister added that Michelle was certainly not a prostitute.

The police were baffled. Literally no one, to their knowledge, had a grudge against Michelle Simms. The impression they had was of a girl who had been in the wrong place at the wrong time, and had been the random choice of victim for a homicidal rapist who stalked his victims in this area.

Four weeks later, on Sunday, 24 June, Elizabeth Laudenbach, a 22-year-old honey blonde who lived at home with her parents in a mobile home, was found dead in an orange grove about ten miles from Tampa. She was nude, and had been shot through the head with a small-calibre handgun.

The media were already referring to the as yet unknown assailant as 'The Sunday Killer', because all the dead girls had been found on a Sunday. But more than fifteen Sundays would elapse before another victim surfaced. She was the first black victim of the Sunday Killer. Eighteen years old, Chanel Williams had left her home in Lake Wales, a small, sleepy rural town in the north of Florida, for the bright lights of Tampa. She had no marketable skills to enable her to secure a job, so she turned to prostitution. On 11 September, only about four weeks after her arrival, she was arrested for soliciting. Unable to pay the fine, she was given a brief jail sentence, after which she was released from the Hillsboro County Jail back on to the streets.

She did not remain on the streets of Tampa for long. On Sunday, 7 October, her nude body was found beside a highway near the Pasco County line. She had been shot through the head. The following Sunday the body of Karen Beth Dinsfriend was recovered from a lake, as has already been described.

The police realized that they had a problem on their hands: the Sunday Killer had already claimed five victims in the space of only six months, all in the Tampa general area. The killer's apparent obsession with Sunday, and the fact that he chose only young women in the 18 to 28 age group, pointed to a pattern, despite the differences in his *modus operandi*, in that some of his victims were bludgeoned or strangled and others shot. All had been raped. Binding them with a cord was also part of the pattern.

If the police had any notion that the Sunday Killer had now ceased his operations, they were in for a nasty shock.

Although the nude and brutalized body of an unidentified, pretty young blonde was discovered beside Highway 301 on a Wednesday, investigating officers surmised that she could very well have been killed on a Sunday, since the pathologist's report on his post-mortem findings indicated that she had been dead for about three days. This victim had been raped and strangled as well as having taken a very severe beating. Police officers had no difficulty in connecting this latest outrage with the MO of the elusive Sunday Killer.

On 3 November police were out in force, swarming all over the Tampa general area in an all-out hunt for the psychopath who had taken six young lives, hoping to find a lead and apprehend him before he could claim yet another victim. Their hope was short-lived. During the search, a missing person report came in. At 2.30 a.m. that morning Richard Wesley, the father of a 17-year-old girl who worked the late shift at a neighbourhood doughnut and coffee shop, had taken a call from her to tell him that she was just leaving and would be home very shortly. The shop was located in a quiet part of Tampa and the father had no qualms about his daughter's practice of walking the few hundred yards home. When she did not arrive at her usual time, however, he became anxious and together with other family members and some neighbours he went out to look for her. Along the route the girl normally took home, they found her white bicycle which she sometimes used, at about 4.40 a.m. As her shift started at a time when other family members were at work, they were not aware which times she cycled and which times she decided to walk, as she used to keep her bike at a nearby friend's house, since her own home had no garden. The bicycle was found lying on its side by the roadside, and not far away was the girl's cosmetic bag, and also a bag of cinnamon doughnuts which she had obviously intended to bring home, as she often did.

The girl, Helen Wesley, was reported missing to the police, and to a newspaper reporter a relative said, 'I think she was taken. She would have had no reason not to come home. She had no boyfriends.' Another relative pointed out that Helen had a condition which required her to take medication three times a day, and did not normally carry more than a day's supply of the pills with her when she went to work. He stressed that if someone were holding her against her will, her physical condition would deteriorate unless she took the pills prescribed for her.

No clue was provided by the manager of the coffee and doughnut shop, who told police: 'I watched her pedal off home on her bike at about 2.30. She was laughing and talking to the other girls. That's the last I saw of her.'

The case took an amazing turn which surprised even the police. At 4.30 a.m. on the Sunday morning Helen turned up at her home, looking and feeling rather the worse for wear. The story she had to tell was an amazing one – of how she had escaped with her life from a man who the police were certain in their own minds was the Sunday Killer.

As she was cycling home, Helen related, a man leapt out from behind a parked van, grabbed her arm and knocked her off her bicycle, saying, 'If you scream I'll kill you.' He manhandled her along and bundled her into his car, which was parked a few feet behind the van. In one hand he held a screwdriver which had been ground to a sharp point. Helen was able to get a good view of her abductor – a stockily built man about 5 ft. 6 in. or so in height, with a shock of thick dark hair, a moustache, and a pudgy face. He wore a gold signet ring on his right hand.

The man then proceeded to blindfold and gag her with strips of what looked like bedsheet material. He then drove for about half an hour until he reached a house, apparently his own, where he bundled the girl inside. There she was held captive until her release.

Helen said that she had been kept gagged and blindfolded. He did not abuse or rape her, and offered to remove the gag if she refrained from making any noise. He even offered her a ham sandwich, which she refused, thinking it might be drugged or poisoned. The man told Helen that he 'liked her a lot' and did not intend to do her any harm, only 'keep her a prisoner for a bit'. He also told her that he was 'old enough to be her father', which was untrue, since although Helen had estimated his age as 35 or so, in the event he was only barely 31. After removing the gag, they had some conversation, during which Helen attempted to find out his motive in keeping her captive. 'Why are you doing this?' she demanded.

'Women keep walking all over me,' he said. 'I hate women. But you seem to be different, so I'm going to let you go. This is my revenge on women. I've done this with other girls.' Helen correctly interpreted the phrase 'I'm going to let you go' to imply that there had been other girls whom he had *not* let go ...

At 3.30 on the Sunday morning he drove her to the vicinity of the place where he had abducted her, after having held her captive for more than twenty-four hours. 'Don't try anything,' the man said. 'I have a gun.' He pressed a small handgun against her head, so that she could feel that it really was a gun, and not just an empty threat. Shortly after this he stopped the car and told her to get out. He ordered her not to remove the blindfold until after she heard him drive off. Since she knew he had a gun, Helen was afraid to remove the blindfold any sooner, so she was unable to see the kind of car her abductor was driving.

Later she was able to give police more details of the man, who was white and, she said, had an educated voice, 'like he could be a college lecturer or something like that'. When she finally took off the blindfold, she found that he had dropped her at a street intersection quite near her home.

The police, now having a fairly good description of the man, stepped up their search for a likely suspect matching his description. Unfortunately they had no description of his car, beyond that it had seemed to be a smallish one – 'a bit cramped inside' – and had what felt like vinyl-upholstered seats. It was also, Helen said, 'a bit noisy' – perhaps this implied that the car was an older model.

If the police thought that the Sunday Killer was now relenting or even getting cold feet as a result of the increased police presence in the area, stopping all cars and questioning any likely looking suspects, they were mistaken. On Tuesday, 6 November, the badly decomposed body of another young woman was found in the Zephyr Hills, in the rural south central part of Pasco

County. On account of the advanced state of decomposition, pathologists were unable to say with any degree of certainty when she had died, nor could they identify her. She was logged only as a while female about 20 years of age.

Less than a week after this body had been found, another corpse was discovered on the afternoon of Monday, 12 November. It was identified as the body of Kim Swann, aged 21, of Tampa. She had been found lying beneath the overpass of Interstate Highway 75 south-east of Tampa. The slender strawberry blonde had been strangled, raped and physically abused. The pathologist stated that she had probably been killed early on the preceding day – Sunday.

A background probe of the victim revealed that Kim was a medical technology student, who spent Saturday nights in the bars along Tampa's Nebraska Avenue strip. She was not known to dabble in drugs, nor was she a heavy drinker. No element of prostitution was involved.

By now the frustrated police decided to pull out all the stops and work round the clock to catch the elusive Sunday Killer. They formed a task force which included investigators from the FBI, the Florida Department of Law Enforcement, Pasco County sheriff's officers and the Tampa police force. They focused their efforts on locating a likely suspect who matched the description Helen Wesley had provided. On the Friday afternoon following the discovery of Kim Swann's body, they spotted a man whose description exactly matched that given by Helen, coming out of a cinema and getting into a small older-model car. They surrounded the car and arrested the driver, 31-year-old Robert Long, an unemployed radiology technician from West Virginia, who had an apartment in Tampa.

In custody, Long admitted that he was the man the police were looking for. County Sheriff Walter Heinrich said later: 'Long did not resist the arresting officers. We are now searching his apartment for evidence.' But the most damning evidence was not to be found in his apartment but in his 1979 Dodge car, which had been given a thorough forensic examination. Some red fibres from the car carpet matched red fibres recovered from the bodies of several of the victims, and Helen Wesley had told investigators that the carpet in the car was red.

Robert Long was charged with eight counts of murder and the abduction of Helen Wesley. He then told investigating officers that in addition to the murders of which he was already accused there was another which should be taken into consideration. He told them that her body could be found in the rural north-eastern part of Hillsboro County, near an uncompleted stretch of the Interstate Highweay 75. Early on the morning of Saturday, 17 November, detectives took Long with them to locate the body in a copse of scrub oak, where Long said he had disposed of the remains of a 21-year-old waitress, Virginia Lee Johnson, from Connecticut. She had worked in a fast-food joint along the Nebraska Avenue Strip in Tampa. She had gone missing in September. Owing to the length of time that had elapsed before her body was found, it was little more than a skeleton when discovered. It was identified from dental work which had been carried out on her teeth, and also from a ring which she always wore.

The waitress worked the night shift – 11 p.m. to 7 a.m. – at the all-night fast-food outlet at which she was employed. At about 10 p.m. on 7 September her next door neighbour reported that Virginia had knocked at her door to ask for a ride to work, saying that she would pop back to shower and change into her working uniform and would be ready in about half an hour. At 11 o'clock, when the neighbour knocked on her door to say she had the car outside, she got no reply.

'I thought she had decided to walk instead,' the neighbour later said. 'She liked walking, and she used to hitch-hike quite a lot. I did think it rather odd, though, that she had not come to tell me she was going to walk instead of going in my car.' When she did not show up for work on two consecutive days and no one had seen her, she was reported missing.

At the coffee and doughnut shop where Helen Wesley had worked, detectives interviewed a number of the regulars. Many of them said that when they saw photographs of Robert Long in the newspapers or on TV news programmes, they recognized him as a man who had frequently hung around the neighbourhood and several times bought doughnuts and coffee. He would sit quietly at a table, taking a long time over his coffee, and stare silently out of the window at the passers-by in the street. 'He was a very quiet sort of guy,' one of them said. 'He would sit by himself and never talked to anybody,' another said. 'But after Helen Wesley was abducted, we never saw him again.'

News of Long's arrest was greeted with relief in the bars and nightclubs on the Nebraska Avenue strip. Waitresses, hostesses and dancers no longer walked in fear or called a cab instead of hitch-hiking. At the club where Peggy Long (no relation to the Sunday Killer) worked, the manager threw a party for everybody to celebrate.

A special court was convened, appropriately enough, on Sunday, 18 November, and Robert Long, handcuffed to two prison officers, was arraigned, in Hillsboro County Jail's small courtroom, on eight counts of first-degree murder, eight counts of sexual battery, and nine counts of kidnapping. A ninth murder count was anticipated to be added by Pasco County authorities.

The following day, Monday, 19 November, a bizarre development occurred while Long was in custody. A fisherman in his boat on the Hillsboro River snagged his line on an object floating near the cypress-fringed bank, just below the surface. It was the body of a woman. She was white, in her late teens or early twenties, very slender, 5 ft. 1 in. in height, with long brown hair and pierced ears but not wearing earrings. An artist's impression of how she might have looked in life was drawn and published in the hope that someone would come forward and identify her.

'The place where she was found,' a police spokesman was to say later, 'was only a few miles from the spot where Chanel Williams's body was discovered, and only a few hundred yards from where we found the body of the victim that Long led us to on Saturday.' The autopsy report made it clear that the girl had been murdered while Robert Long was still at large. She had been garrotted with a cord which was digging tightly into her neck and partly-embedded in the flesh. An appendectomy scar on her abdomen would, perhaps, aid in identification, as also would a tattoo above her left breast. These identifying details were included in the description published alongside the artist's impression.

The same day that these were appearing in the newspapers, a woman came forward to say that she knew the victim. Taken in a police car to the morgue, she identified the body as that of Kimberly Kylie Hopps, 23, who had a record of arrests for prostitution and for being drunk and disorderly. Long confessed also to this murder, saying that 'he hated whores'. When police interrogators pointed out that several of his victims were not prostitutes, Lond shrugged and said that he hated women in general and whores in particular.

Following his indictment, Long was taken to Dade County Court, in Dade City, to face the first of nine couts of murder, the tenth victim's case being left on file. Prior to his trial before Judge Raymond E. Ulmer, Long offered to plead guilty to the kidnapping, rape and murder of Virginia Lee Johnson in exchange for a waiver of the death penalty. The plea-bargaining bid was refused. Assistant District Attorney Philip Van Allen said: 'I'm going to see him in the electric chair, even if I have to try him separately on each of the nine murders to ensure that he'll fry for one of them.'

The security around the courtroom at the trial was like Fort Knox. Anyone entering the court was passed through a metal detector which was sensitive enough to respond to aluminium foil on a cigarette pack.

Predictably, since Long had confessed to all the murders, the defence had no possible way of saying that Long had not committed them, so they had no choice but to put in an insanity plea in mitigation. They also challenged the prosecution's declaration that the murders were premeditated.

'Of course they were premeditated!' Van Allen averred. 'He took his victims, bound, gagged and naked, in his car to isolated rural locations. He beat, battered, raped and strangled them. He then concealed their bodies, hid or destroyed their clothes, and left the scene. If that is not premeditation, what is? He went out in his car prowling around looking for random victims. It simply screams premeditation!'

The jury took just forty-four minutes to find Robert Long guilty on each of the nine counts of murder in the first degree, as well as all the other charges of aggravated sexual battery and kidnapping. Long showed no emotion on hearing the verdict. He shrugged nonchalantly, winked at some of the spectators, and left the court whistling.

When the jury returned for the penalty phase, defence attorney Robert Norgard turned to the subject of serial killers:

> Serial murder is a disease which few people understand. Studies of other serial killers, like Ted Bundy and John Wayne Gacy, indicate that the murderers' personalities are similar. It is frightening how Mr Long compares to these people. By executing these individuals, in no way can society benefit from their mistakes ... When you talk to Mr Long, there's chaos, no internal order at all. To execute this individual would be cruel and inhuman, in the light of his condition. I'd like to think society has gone further than to execute people with mental problems.

Prosecutor Van Allen, referring to a defence psychiatrist's testimony that Long was insane, said: 'I submit to you that they are operating under the preconceived idea that anybody who would commit a murder as cruel [as these] has to be crazy. That simply is not the law.'

The jury were out less than half an hour before returning a verdict that Long should be sentenced to death for his crimes with no mitigating circumstances. Judge Ulmer pronounced sentence as Long stood before him showing no sign of emotion. 'In keeping with my responsibility,' the judge said, 'I accept the jury's unanimous recommendations. The aggravating circumstances outweigh any mitigating circumstances.' The judge then read the formal legal sentence that Long 'should be electrocuted until you are dead', and prepared the death warrant to be signed by the Governor of the

State of Florida. He ended by addressing Long: 'May God have mercy on your soul.'

Long, with the typical indifference of the psychopath, simply shrugged, and when asked if he had anything to say, remained mute. He was then led from the court by court bailiffs, to be taken to Raiford Penitentiary, where he still languishes on death row as he awaits his date with Old Sparky.

12

A Dustbin Full of Guts

Michael Yarbrough (1985)

Thursday, 16 May 1985 was just a normal working day for the refuse disposal men in Las Vegas, Nevada as they went about their business emptying dustbins in one of the downtown areas of the city. The work started early in the morning – six o'clock saw them well into their task. The sanitation department believed in an early start to the day so that the workmen who had one of the most unpleasant jobs of all could knock off early, take a shower at their depot, don a change of clean clothes from their lockers and go home.

At 7.15 a.m. a call came in to their dispatcher's office reporting a grisly find in one of the dustbins ranged along the wall of an industrial building facing on to an alley. The caller was a veteran of the Vietnam war who had come upon a small group of street people who were out early to scavenge in the bins. They appeared to be fighting over something contained in one of the bins. 'What's all the commotion about?' he asked a woman who was not actually involved in the squabble. 'It's a ham,' she replied. 'Some idiot has thrown out a whole ham – must want their brains testing! Fresh, too – no old mouldy stuff.'

The Nam veteran edged his way into the mêlée and took a look. 'That's no ham!' he observed aloud. From his war experiences he knew what he was looking at – it was the upper portion of a man's thigh. While the drifters and transients still fought over the supposed 'ham' he went to the nearest telephone booth to call police. He could see the crowd still fighting over their find – they had completely ignored his observation and probably thought he was joking.

Officers Bob Leonard and Norman Ziola were soon at the scene, quickly dispersed the crowd and ordered the alley behind 611 Las Vegas Boulevard North roped off, much to the annoyance of the disappointed scavengers who loudly expressed their protests at being deprived of their supposed 'ham'. 'If we'd told them what it was,' Bob said to his partner later, 'they'd all have run a mile!'

The sanitation department's Silver State Disposal Service informed the investigating officers that all the dustbins had been emptied at 6.15 that morning in that section of the city and the refuse taken to the city dump. Police searched the dump, but no other body parts were found. They also meticulously searched the other bins in the area without result. The bin in which the thigh had been found was taken away for forensic examination. Officers Leonard and Ziola questioned the war veteran further. 'I know what a ham looks like,' he told them. 'I told the people there it wasn't a ham, but they took not the slightest notice.' Police calculated that the thigh had been dumped in the bin about an hour after the rubbish had been collected, but before the scavengers arrived.

The thigh, wrapped in white plastic, was that of a white male, and appeared to have been recently severed, according to the pathologist's report. There was scarcely any trace of blood inside the plastic bag, which indicated that the thigh had been drained of blood before being wrapped and disposed of. The identity of the victim remained a mystery. Still more mysterious was the identity of the man who had murdered and dismembered him.

Meanwhile, the sewage disposal men were busy at the treatment plant on West Cheyenne Avenue. One of the workmen's duties was to scrape the metal filter screen with a rubber squeegee to separate the raw sewage sludge from extraneous objects. On infrequent occasions watches, even diamond rings, had come through, most

likely dropped down the toilet by some mischievous
toddler. But what the filter screen worker saw coming
through now was no diamond ring, or even a watch. Two
objects, dead white, looked exactly like human fingers.
The workman took a second, closer look. 'My God!' he
stammered, almost falling back against the supporting
wall of the filtering chamber. 'Get the supervisor!' he
shouted up to the worker above the filtering chamber.
Within minutes the supervisor, clad in rubber boots,
climbed down into the chamber and waded across the
sludge to the filter outlet. By this time yet another object
had come through. This was not another finger, but a
human penis! The first man had an uncontrollable urge to
vomit, but the supervisor was made of sterner stuff. Very
soon they were in the dispatcher's office talking to the
police on their emergency hotline.

'Switch off the pipeline which enters the filtering
chamber,' an officer instructed them. 'Don't touch
anything. We will have someone out there in five
minutes'.

At police headquarters, the officer who had taken the
call was reporting to Lieutenant John Conner, the head of
the homicide department. 'More body parts have turned
up,' he said. 'Two fingers and a *penis*, would you believe!'

'Where?'

'At the sewage treatment plant on West Cheyenne
Avenue.'

Lieutenant Conner looked at the large-scale wall map of
the city, from which he observed that the sewage
treatment plant was several miles from the alley where the
plastic-wrapped thigh had been found in the dustbin. He
realized that a psychopathic killer was on the loose,
chopping up a body, or bodies, and dumping the parts in
various places all over the city.

While squads of police officers searched the city for a
lead to the identity of the victim and that of the killer,
officers were deployed to remain at the sewage filter
chamber to see whether any more body parts had come
through, apparently flushed down a toilet somewhere in
the vast sprawling maze of the city's streets. Their
patience was rewarded. By four o'clock that afternoon

more parts had surfaced: a pair of lips, a nose, two ears, and a portion of scalp with hair attached. In short order these gruesome finds were cleaned of sewage sludge and laid out for the pathologist's inspection on one of the stainless steel autopsy tables, alongside the thigh, the two fingers and the penis, at the city morgue.

The pathologist stated that he would have to wait for the results of the blood grouping tests to enable him to confirm his findings, but so far he could tell the police that the texture and colour of the skin of the various parts would seem to point to their having all come from the same body. He said that, judging by the size of the portion of thighbone found in the thigh, the victim was probably about 5ft. 9in. tall, and of fairly stocky build. His hair was dark brown and wavy. Beyond this he could not go, but asked about the probable age of the victim, he estimated that he was in his mid thirties or slightly older. When eventually the blood grouping test results came through, he was able to confirm that all the parts had indeed come from the same body. He added that the dismemberment had been carried out by a person with little or no knowledge of anatomy, using a very blunt instrument such as a table knife or a wide-toothed saw.

Detective Ziola asked the pathologist whether it would be possible to obtain fingerprints from the two fingers that had been found in the sewage filter chamber. He said that the fingers would have to be soaked in a chemical solution to expand the shrivelled skin first, but they had been recently severed and so the flesh was not decomposed. Thus it would be possible to lift fingerprints from them, since the ends of the fingers – a right index and middle finger, sawn off at the first joint – were intact. This process was carried out and the two fingerprints successfully lifted. A search of police records showed that there was no one with identical prints in their files – in other words, the victim had no criminal record.

At eight o'clock the next morning, Friday, 17 May, a call came through to police headquarters and the message was quickly relayed to Lieutenant Conner. The call had scarcely been logged when a squad car full of police officers sped to a location on the 200 block of Seventh

Avenue, where they found a half-drunken vagrant, clad in filthy rags and clutching a bottle of booze in his hand, sitting on the pavement propped up against the wall. He looked as though he had seen a ghost; a deathly pallor showed through the grime.

'In there!' he croaked, pointing with a trembling finger to a dustbin not far away. 'The dustbin's full of guts!'

Two of the officers walked across to the trash dumpster and pushed open the metal top. Inside was a two-gallon white plastic bucket, full to the top with what were obviously human intestines. The stench and the sight combined to make both officers vomit. There is a limit to what even experienced policemen can stomach, and they were no rookies.

A call was put through from the radio in the cruiser to Lieutenant Conner, and within minutes Detectives Ziola and Leonard had arrived at the scene, followed by the police lab transport van and two lab technicians. The bucket with its noisome contents was lifted gingerly into the van for transport to the pathologist's department.

The vagrant was taken to the police station and given hot coffee and sandwiches and his booze confiscated. He was also given a hot shower and some clean clothes from the police stores. Having somewhat recovered, he was then asked to make a statement. He said that he discovered the bucket of guts when he flipped open the lid of the dumpster to look for discarded aluminium cans to collect the deposits. He had then told a passer-by of his find, and this man had called the police. The vagrant was then given a dollar from police funds for a haircut and shave, and provided with the address of a hostel for homeless alcoholics.

Police cordoned off the area, which was just one block from the alley where the thigh had been found. They considered this to be significant, as it seemed to indicate that the perpetrator of this ghastly outrage lived in the vicinity. The officers searched the area but found no more body parts. The dustbin contained a good deal of blood, and there was blood on the wall nearby and on the pavement. Close to the bin was a shoe print in blood; this was photographed, and bloodstained refuse still in the bin was taken away along with the bin itself for forensic examination.

Meanwhile, detectives were making intensive door-to-door inquiries asking for details of anyone who might have mysteriously gone missing in the past forty-eight hours or so, who matched the tentative description of a white male of stocky build, about 5ft. 9in. tall, with brown hair. A possible lead developed when the manager of a residential hotel on South Sixth Street told the investigators that their profile sounded rather like his security guard, Dexter Evans, aged 36, who worked for him part time shooing the drunks and loiterers off his front steps. 'He did a good job,' the manager said, 'but inevitably he made some enemies. Sometimes he got into a fight with some bum. He worked nights. One morning he came in with a right shiner. He also told me that he had been threatened several times that someone or other would "get him" or "do him". He was certainly not popular.'

Asked about his absence, he had not turned up for work for several days, which, the manager said, was most unusual for him – in fact it was quite out of character. If he was off sick he would call in. So the manager was beginning to think that some harm had indeed befallen him. The manager had last seen him alive at 2 a.m. standing on the steps outside the hotel on the previous Sunday.

Back at headquarters, the officers ran a computer check on the missing security guard. Evans had no criminal record, and did not own or drive a car. He had no known relatives in the area. He could very well have fallen foul of one of the street bums he had moved on from the vicinity of his employer's premises. And he did at least fit the description which the pathologist had tentatively offered.

Meanwhile, at the scene where the dustbin with its ghastly contents had been found, Officers Ziola and Leonard were assiduously searching every inch of the ground near the place where it had stood. The presence of blood on the wall, and a bloody shoe print on the adjoining pavement, led them to speculate that there was more than just a likelihood that the murderer lived in the vicinity and had dumped the various body parts conveniently near to his abode to avoid carrying them around the city. The small parts he had flushed down the toilet would be carried some miles out through the sewer system. It was odd that only two fingers had turned up, though – after all, fingers were a vital part of a corpse from the identification point of view, and if these could be disposed of it would render a connection between the killer and his victim less likely. Or so he thought ...

A body could scarcely be identified from half a thigh. But officers asked one another: where was the torso? Where was the head? Where were the rest of the legs, and the arms?

As Detectives Ziola and Leonard continued their examination of the area, they noticed another police officer on his hands and knees closely scrutinizing the ground in the cordoned-off area behind them. They went over to him.

'Look at this!' Officer Daniel Harkness said, pointing to a faint trail of browning stains which ran along close to the wall in the direction of the next dustbin, about twenty yards from the site where the first one had stood before it had been removed. The trail was unmistakably dried blood, although faint and discoloured both by dust and by the length of time that had elapsed since it had been made. It led directly to the dustbin. Peering inside after flipping the lid open, Ziola and Leonard discovered two men's shirts and a pair of men's trousers, all heavily bloodstained, a bloody necktie, rags and newspapers, all blood-soaked, which could have been used in mopping-up operations by the killer, and a human lower jaw with teeth still embedded in the bone. The wall behind the dumpster was splashed and smeared with blood, as also was the side of the bin itself.

Further examination revealed that the blood-trail continued on the opposite side of the bin and led to the rear of a prefabricated bungalow which fronted the 200 block of South Seventh Street. While assistance was radioed for to remove the bin and its contents to the forensic laboratory, Ziola and Leonard walked across a wooden walkway made of planks which lay across a drainage ditch at the rear of the bungalow. They knocked loudly at the door. 'Open up! Police!' Someone was heard rummaging around and walking with heavy footsteps towards the door. 'Yeah? Who is it?' The voice sounded like that of a man who had just awakened from a heavy sleep.

'Police. Open up!' the officers repeated, this time more authoritatively.

The door eventually opened, and an unkempt-looking man, who appeared to be in his late 30s or early 40s, appeared, clad in a plaid work shirt and blue jeans. He had thick, dishevelled brown hair and an ill-trimmed moustache and sideburns. 'Come in, fellas,' he offered. 'What's this all about?'

The officers were non-committal and told him that they wanted to take him in for questioning. He was Michael Harvey Yarbrough, 33, a native of Alabama, who had been living in Las Vegas for eight months. He shared the clapboard bungalow with two room-mates, Jim Logan, aged 41, and Paul Fogarty, 36. Logan was out looking for work, Yarbrough said and would be back at any time. The other man was also unemployed – in fact all three of them were – and had gone out on the morning of Wednesday, 15 May, saying he was going to look for a job. That, Yarbrough said, was the last time he had set eyes on him. He had no idea where he might be, but opined that he could have gone to stay at the home of one or other of his friends.

Shortly after one o'clock Logan returned, where he found Yarbrough in conversation with the two policemen. He volunteered some additional information. He had not found a job, but had come back simply to have some food and then go out job-hunting again. Yes, he had seen Paul Fogarty on Wednesday morning, just as Yarbrough had told them.

While Yarbrough was taken out to the cruiser, Logan was questioned more closely. 'Did you see Paul Fogarty again after that Wednesday morning?' Ziola asked.

'No.' He said, when he got back that evening from job-hunting, he found the door locked from the inside and bolted, because he could not open the door with his key. He banged on the door for admission. 'Mike answered without opening the door,' Logan said. 'He said he couldn't let me in right then and asked me to come back later.'

'Did you not think that rather strange?'

'Yes, I did,' replied Logan, but I didn't attach too much significance to it. Mike could have had any number of reasons for not wanting me there at that particular time.'

'What happened then, when you went back later that night?'

'Mike told me that Paul had been taken to jail for threatening the landlord with a chopper,' he said. 'I thought that was a bit strange, too. Paul was not an aggressive kind of guy, and as far as I know he had always gotten on well with the landlord.'

'You never saw Paul again?'

'No.'

Yarbrough, in the cruiser, was handcuffed to a detective, but still not told what the arrest was about. 'You'll find out soon enough,' he was told.

At police headquarters, Lieutenant Conner, informed of the developments, contacted District Attorney Thomas Miller and told him that his officers had arrested a suspect in the 'Body Parts' case and required a search warrant for his home. The DA replied that there would be no problem and that he would come over to police headquarters and deliver it personally. In short order he arrived with the search warrant – it was barely two o'clock – and four detectives were detailed to search the clapboard bungalow from top to bottom.

In the meantime, forensic experts had obtained dental records for the missing security guard and compared them with the teeth in the jawbone which had been found in the dumpster. They did not match and the security guard was eliminated as a suspected victim. Dental records were unobtainable for Paul Fogarty, who was said to be a native of Detroit, but detectives were pretty certain in their own minds that the victim whose body parts had been found was in fact Paul Fogarty.

At the bungalow, the searchers found bloodstains on the floor and walls of the bathroom, the toilet and the bathtub, as well as on the windows of the kitchen and on the floor leading out of the house. Among items found at the house and confiscated were three knives, two handsaws and a chopper, as well as bloodstained clothing, boots and gloves. No further body parts were found.

Yarbrough was charged with first-degree murder of Paul Fogarty and booked into Clark County jail. Asked where the torso, head, and the rest of the body was, he replied, 'I don't know what you guys are talking about. I haven't done anything but look for work, and that's not a crime.'

A week later, Dr James Clark, the pathologist, had prepared his report on the bucket of intestines found in the dumpster. They had, he said, most likely come from the same person whose other body parts he had examined, and were all of the same blood group. The likelihood was that the victim was Paul Fogarty. The colour of the hair attached to the scalp was the same as his, and the estimated height of the man whose thigh bone he had measured would correspond more or less with that of Fogarty, who had been 5ft. 9in. tall. At the preliminary hearing on 12 June, the pathologist testified that all the body parts had come from the same body, and showed similar wounds made by blunt instruments in crudely severing them from the body. Furthermore, he testified that fingerprints taken from the two fingers which had surfaced at the sewage plant matched fingerprints lifted from Paul Fogarty's possessions at the home which he shared with Yarbrough and Logan.

Several days later, Yarbrough suddenly decided to confess. He told police investigators that the murder was 'getting to him' and that he wanted to get it off his chest. But he refused to say anything about the whereabouts of the victim's torso, head and other missing body parts. 'I cut him up, packaged him, put him in a supermarket trolley and delivered him,' he said. 'I didn't want to kill him,' he continued, 'but he was coming at me with a hatchet. It was either him or me. It was self-defence.'

The trial began before Judge Stephen Huffaker in October 1985. The courtroom was packed to capacity, with people queuing outside trying unsuccessfully to gain admission after all the available seats were filled. Standing was not allowed. The unemployed drifter had no attorney, so one was appointed for him by the court. This was Public Defender Robert Amundsen, who pleaded for leniency. He told the court that the victim, Paul Fogarty, had mental problems, flew off the handle and threatened to kill the defendant with a hatchet for no reason that anyone knows of, on the morning of 15 May. 'The defendant did kill Fogarty,' the attorney said, 'but it was unplanned.'

Prosecutor David Schwartz took a different view. 'This murder was anything but justifiable,' he said. 'It was premeditated, deliberate, cold-blooded and sadistic. It is one of this city's most gruesome murders.'

The jury was subjected to five days of testimony regarding the dismembering of the body, the flushing of parts down the toilet to be found at the sewage works outlet, and the dumping of parts in various dustbins in the downtown part of the city. They did not learn of the final destination of the torso, head and other missing parts, which remains a mystery to this day. Yarbrough is not talking. It may be that, in this way, he feels that he has 'put one over' on the police.

When Yarbrough was called to the witness-stand, he described killing his room-mate in self-defence during an argument which had cropped up during which Fogarty 'came at him with a hatchet'. He then described how he cut up the body in the bath and drained it of most of the blood to facilitate his disposal of the body. He then stated how he went to a local supermarket and took a quantity of plastic bags and a trolley to assist him with the disposal problem. He described how he put the intestines into a plastic bucket and dropped it into a bin some way along the rear alley behind his home, and put part of a leg into another bin, after which he tossed his bloodstained clothing into yet a third bin together with part of the jaw of his victim. But he steadfastly refused to say where the missing parts were, stating that he was 'spaced out' at the time and 'could not remember'.

Yarbrough stated that his worst moment was when his room-mate Jim Logan returned home from job-hunting and asked to be admitted on being unable to open the door. Yarbrough had bolted the door from the inside against just such an eventuality.

Under cross-examination by prosecutor David Schwartz, Yarbrough was asked why, after killing Fogarty, he had cut up his body. Yarbrough replied that he did not have a car and could not drive, so he had to think of some alternative method of disposing of it. The body was too big to get rid of in one piece, so he had to dismember it – he did not really have much choice. He added that he was physically sick several times during these operations, and that he did not really want to chop up his room-mate. Asked why he had cut off the various parts he had flushed down the toilet, the defendant replied, 'I don't remember doing that, but if you found them then I must have done. I was really spaced out.'

'When you say you were "spaced out", do you mean that you were on drugs?' the prosecutor asked.

'No, sir. I never use drugs,' Yarbrough replied.

The jury began their deliberations at 2.30 p.m. on Friday 21 October. They took seven hours to reach a unanimous verdict of guilty of murder in the first degree. Thus Yarbrough's self-defence mitigation plea was tossed out of the window. Yarbrough showed no visible reaction to the verdict, but stood talking quietly with his attorney while the case was adjourned for the penalty phase until 22 November, and then taken back to prison.

At that hearing, again before Judge Huffaker, the eight-man four-woman jury rejected the prosecutor's plea for the death sentence on account of the gruesome nature of the crime. Instead, they embraced the plea made by Public Defender Robert Amundsen that Yarbrough be given a life sentence with some possibility of parole after a reasonable period, so that he might have some chance of atoning for his crime and re-entering society again and leading a decent life. The judge finally pronounced sentence of life in prison, with the proviso that he must serve twenty years before he would be eligible to apply for parole.

Michael Yarbrough is at present incarcerated in Nevada State Prison in Carson City. In the year 2005, when he is 53, he will be eligible to apply for parole. He still maintains a stubborn silence with regard to the whereabouts of the missing torso, head and other body parts of his victim.

13

The Snuff Movie Murder

Geoffrey Jones (1986)

Many sick perverts will go to any lengths to see their sexual fantasies on film. There is a thriving trade in video nasties to cater for their revolting proclivities. In some cases, these mentally disturbed persons enjoy watching simulated killings on film. This is bad enough, but when such a film-maker decides to dispense with the simulation and film a real murder, then the bounds of depravity are exceeded. The cult of the so-called 'snuff movie', taken thus to its most extreme frontiers, is, fortunately, a rare occurrence, but when such a film has been made and word gets around on the grapevine, those sick individuals who have the financial resources available will seek avidly for copies of the video. Needless to say, this will be very hard to come by, for obvious reasons.

One such film-maker was Geoffrey Jones, a 49-year-old bachelor, who lived at 16 Eggington Road, Hall Green, Birmingham. On the afternoon of 18 April 1985 he lured a pretty 17-year-old girl named Marion Terry to his home, on the pretext of offering her a modelling job which he had advertised on a card in a newsagent's shop window. Within fifteen minutes of entering Jones's house, the unsuspecting teenager was dead. She had been hanged during a scene Jones was shooting on video for a film entitled *Enough Rope*.

The full, bizarre story emerged during the four-day trial

which opened on 21 April 1986 at Birmingham Crown Court before judge Sir Joseph Cantley. The jury of eight men and four women were visibly shocked as they listened to the gruesome details of how a normal, fun-loving, attractive teenager had met a horrendous death at the hands of a man whom the prosecuting counsel described as 'a monster in human form'.

Brian Escott Cox QC, described in his opening speech as prosecutor how Marion Terry, who had been unemployed, lived with her parents in Cole Valley Road, Hall Green, Birmingham. On the afternoon of 18 April 1985 she had been out looking for a job when she spotted the card in the newsagent's shop window advertising a job as a model. The card stated, 'Wanted – Young lady for part-time modelling. Experience not necessary.' This was followed by Jones's name, address and telephone number. When Marion rang Jones, he asked her to come round to his home wearing 'something black'. This she did.

Jones, Mr Cox continued, had written a film script entitled *Enough Rope*, in which a young girl hanged herself. Jones explained the script to the girl and took her to his loft, which he had fitted out as a studio with his video recorder and various ropes, including a noose suspended from a hook in the ceiling, underneath which was a chair. He told the girl to stand on the chair and to place the noose, which appeared to be a length of ordinary clothes line, around her neck. She refused, and a struggle ensued. Jones forced the noose over her head and pulled the chair from under her feet, leaving her to hang, while the camera recorded every detail of her death throes.

Some hours afterwards, Mr Cox said, Jones was seen by neighbours driving away from his home, having placed a package in his car. It was believed by the police that he was in all likelihood going to dispose of the film, either by post or by leaving it in the custody of a trusted associate.

'You may be asking yourselves,' Mr Cox told the jury, 'how he was able to contact young girls and enjoy these sexual fantasies. The answer is that he is an amateur film-maker and he advertised for models. Some young girls get carried away by the idea of becoming a model or film star. It certainly worked in Jones's case.' Mr Cox stated that Jones had declared himself to be a keen supporter of capital punishment by hanging. As he looked across at the prisoner in the dock, he added: 'No doubt his present predicament has watered down his views about that.'

On the second day of the trial, evidence was given that Jones had claimed that he had tried to resuscitate his victim after finding that she had accidentally hanged herself during the fiming of a 'mock' hanging scene. Detective Chief Inspector Barry McKay of Birmingham CID described an interview he had had with the accused:

> Jones told me that Marion was posing standing on a chair with the noose around her neck, which she had slipped over her head herself. She then asked Jones to go and fetch her handbag which she had left in the bathroom as she wanted to comb her hair before he filmed the shot. He did so, and when he returned to the attic he found that the chair had slipped and the girl was hanging. He claimed that when he tried to undo the knot in the noose, she bit his fingers and kicked him.

This interview had taken place after Jones had been released from Solihull General Hospital, where he had been taken after an alleged suicide bid. He had reportedly swallowed 100 aspirin tablets, but after his stomach was pumped out he was released into police custody. Jones himself next went into the witness-box to state his case.

Jones described how he had advertised for a model on a card in a newsagent's shop window. Marion had responded, and he had agreed to pay her £10 per hour as her modelling fee plus an additional £50 when the film, *Enough Rope*, had been completed. He admitted that he did not at first inform Marion that she was to be asked to take part in a hanging stunt for the film, but told her only after she was in his attic studio. 'After all,' Jones said, 'no girl in her right mind would go to the house of a chap she didn't know from Adam, stand on a chair and put her head into a noose.'

When they came to the part of the film where the girl had to hang herself, Jones continued, Marion stood on the chair and put the noose around her neck perfectly willingly. It was at this point that she told him that she wanted to comb her hair before the shot was filmed, and asked him to fetch her handbag, which she had left in the bathroom downstairs. According to Jones, it was while he was downstairs getting the bag that he heard a bump. He rushed upstairs and found the teenager hanging, with the chair about two feet away from her feet. Jones expressed the opinion that he was unable to tell whether the hanging had been an accident or whether the girl had deliberately kicked the chair away in order to experience what a real hanging would feel like, possibly in the belief that it might produce a sexual thrill.

Jones then related how he had tried to revive the girl when he found her hanging. She was not dead, he said, because when he grabbed her by the feet to try to lift her body, she kicked him in the chest. He then tried to loosen the knot, but she bit his fingers. She started to make gurgling noises and then went limp, and he realized that she was dead. He said that he went into the bathroom as he felt sick. When he returned, he could not believe that the hanging had been for real and that his model had died. At that point, he said, he switched off the video cmaera and sat on a chair – the same chair on which the girl had stood – to decide what he should do. the body was about two feet from him. He decided that the best way out of his dilemma would be to commit suicide.

Accordingly, said the accused, he went to the house of a close woman friend, who had been out walking her dog and had only just returned to find Jones on her doorstep, in a very agitated state. He told her that a girl had died in his house, and he was sobbing. He said the girl had come to his house in response to an advertisement to do a film stunt and that he had accidentally killed her during the course of filming. He said that he had taken a hundred aspirins, because he deserved to die.

The next witness was the woman friend, who related that they were not lovers in the accepted sense because Jones was impotent. 'We have never had any sexual relationship,' she told the court, 'because he told me he is not capable. He told me that he does not get any feelings of sexual excitement.' If she had believed him, no on else in the courtroom did ...

The idea that Marion Terry could have been experimenting to see whether the sensation of hanging produced any sexual feelings was refuted by the victim's boyfriend, Brian Wilcox, a 19-year-old college student:

Marion was a normal girl and certainly had no such bizarre fantasies. We were planning to marry after I had completed my studies and got a job. She was unemployed after leaving school and I can quite understand that she would have jumped at the chance of earning money as a model, although I think she was foolish to go into the house of a man she did not know who advertised on cards – it was not as if it were a well-known film company advertising in the newspaper. Still, I did not know she was going there, or I would have warned her of the risk involved that this was some weirdo.

Asked whether he considered the death of Marion Terry to have been an accident, he replied, 'I don't think so. She would have been too careful to let such a thing happen.'

The next witness was an ambulance controller, Michelle Green, who had logged in a call from the accused's woman friend, who told her that Jones was 'in a bad way' in her house, having told her that he had taken a hundred aspirins in a bid to commit suicide, and that he would rather die in her home than in his own house in which there was a dead body.

At the hospital, Jones was recorded as having said, 'I am sorry to give you all this bother. I went to my friend's house to die, but she sent for you. I have also killed a young girl. Her body is in my house.' Miss Green then told him that that was a matter for the police, not the hospital authorities, who then called police to take Jones's statement, which in essence was the same as that he had given to the hospital staff.

The third day of the trial was taken up with the evidence of witnesses who had modelled in the past for Jones. Christina Attner, aged 26, had starred in a film he had made entitled *Safety Last*. Jones staged a grisly première at his home to show the film, at which he added a bizarre touch by hiring a girl to act as an usherette, selling ice lollies. Christina's mother and husband were invited to this showing, and were ushered into a darkened room in which rows of chairs accommodated some twenty people, mostly men. The film showed Christina narrowly missing death under the wheels of a train, being apparently run over by a bus, and finally being hanged. At that time, the witness said, the modeling fee was only £2 per hour. Her mother and her husband were aware that she was starring in the gruesome film. They voiced no objection when she told them that she was going to be auditioned for the film in a private house by a man who was advertising, under the name of 'Kit Arden Productions', on shop-window cards.

Christina described to the court Jones's various procedures during the filming. First of all he filmed her, wearing black figure-hugging dresses, at his home. He then took her to a railway siding in his car. There he placed her between the buffers of two stationary engines and filmed her being apparently crushed. Jones told her to assume expressions of abject terror on her face, but not to scream, for fear of attracting attention. He told her that he would dub in screams later when editing the film.

For the bus scene he took her to a bus depot where buses stood which were out of service or in need of repairs. He told her to lie beneath the wheels of a large double-decker: 'It was really scary', she admitted. Again she had to simulate extreme terror but not scream, so as to avoid bringing bus cleaning staff or mechanics running to the scene.

Finally, for the climax of the film, Christina had to simulate a self-hanging. She told the court:

He asked me to stand on a chair and put a noose round my neck. I was told to put my head on one side so as to look as if my neck had been broken. Then he got me to climb up the wall to reach a sort of ledge, where I had to cling on with my fingers, leaving my legs dangling. He then filmed my feet as I dangled. It was rather a difficult scene to do as the ledge was rather high up on the wall. I had to redo it several times before he got it right. I got the distinct impression that he was enjoying all this very much, but I was not enjoying it at all.

The court was also told that Jones had taken a number of still photographs of Christine wearing a tight black dress.

Another model, 25-year-old Dawn Chambers, told the court that she had starred in a film made by Jones called *Ten Little Beauty Queens*, illustrating his version of the popular rhyme, in which ten beautiful young girls each meet an horrific death. She, too, was paid £2 an hour for her modelling fee. Neither Miss Chambers nor Miss Attner received a bonus payment after the film was completed; instead, each received some free tickets to admit family members or friends to the first showing. Again, these performances were held at his house.

The fourth and last day of the trial saw Mr Cox again in action as he made his closing speech to the jury. He totally rejected Jones's version of events, saying that his story was 'preposterous'. 'You will have to try to get inside the warped mind of this man and try to understand his bizarre fantasies,' Mr Cox told the jury. 'Only then will you be able to see how he could have carried out such a dreadful deed.'

Mr Cox described Jones as a man with very severe sexual problems and the most extreme perversions:

Almost certainly, he cannot perform the normal sexual act. He obtains sexual pleasure and relief from fantasies about young girls in danger of death. His greatest enjoyment is that of visualizing young girls clad in skin-tight black clothing, terror-stricken in a situation of life-threatening danger.

He went on to state that Jones had admitted to an admiration for Hitler, and said that he was obsessed with black magic, the occult, and Nazi war atrocities, about which he had a sizeable library at his home:

His principal delight is in hanging, and to hang a young girl was the ultimate fantasy which he turned into reality on the eighteenth day of April 1985. He lied to the police and to the hospital staff that it had been an accident. That is pure rubbish. He killed her in a struggle to force her to put the noose around her neck as she stood on a chair. In that struggle she bit his fingers, which was proved by doctors at the hospital and also by police photographs of his injured fingers, which were consistent with human bites. It is true that he took an overdose of aspirin, but the suicide bid was as fake as some of the scenes in his films. Doctors who treated him have stated that the amount of aspirin he took was minimal and would not have killed anybody.

Jones, who sat quietly in the dock, listened without visible signs of emotion as Mr Cox continued.

He had made several other films before the final one during the making of which Miss Terry died. He wrote sick sexual fantasies into the scripts for these productions, in which Miss Attner, Miss Chambers and two other girls diced with death while enacting hanging scenes at Jones's home, until his ultimate fantasy came true with the hanging of Miss Terry in a real-life snuff movie.

Cox looked intently at the jury.

It is open to question, how many other young girls have literally taken their lives in their hands at the mercy of this monster in human form. We shall not know, for no others have come forward, and Jones is not telling.

The jury took only an hour to find Jones guilty of murder, and Jones showed no reaction as the judge, Sir Joseph Cantley, pronounced sentence of life imprisonment. Asked if he had anything to say, the prisoner made no reply.

After the case, it was revealed that Jones had been having psychiatric treatment for depression following the death of his mother. But the main topic of conversation in the courtroom after the case had ended was speculation as to what had happened to the real-life snuff movie.

Police were certain that Jones had filmed Marion Terry's death throes in his attic studio. They contend that he

could either have posted the film to an accomplice –
possibly another member of the pornographic video
network – or he could have driven to the home of an
associate to entrust it to him. A third option was that he
could have hidden it in some 'safe' place, though this they
considered to be less likely, in case it fell into
unauthorized hands. He was known to have driven off
with a package in his car a few hours after the girl's death,
and before returning home and visiting his friend with the
story of his suicide bid.

Detective Chief Inspector Barry McKay is quoted as
saying:

> We shall never know exactly what Jones did while that
> poor girl was strung up for all those hours. It is absolute
> rubbish for him to say that he tried to revive her – no
> attempt whatsoever was made to cut her down. Mr Cox
> produced the noose in court and anyone could see that it
> had not been cut at all. I am convinced that Jones
> continued to film her as she was hanging there.
> Afterwards I think he went to conceal the film, the
> intention being to retrieve it after his eventual release.

Jones's mail was intercepted after his arrest and
scrutinized for months, but no clue ever emerged as to the
whereabouts of the snuff movie. But even his letters from
jail still harp on his fascination with girls clad entirely in
black, although predictably he made no mention of
hanging fantasies. His former woman friend wrote to him
in prison to say that she wished to end their association,
which is understandable enough. Christina Attner wrote
to him saying that she had decided to give up modelling,
as one close shave was more than enough. 'That girl might
have been me,' she said.

Jones replied, in part: 'It might have been, but it wasn't.
Still, in a way, it's all been a bit of a giggle. But I knew that
in the end I would have to pay the price for the good
times.'

Good times? All a bit of a giggle? You must be kidding.

14

A Cannibal in Texas

Kenneth Stogsdill (1986)

On the morning of Thursday, 4 April 1975, a man stood at
the side of the road on Highway 286 near Wichita Falls, in
western Texas. He was frantically waving his arms, but he
was no ordinary hitch-hiker. He was trying to attract the
attention of a police car. Eventually a Highway Patrol
vehicle appeared on the scene and screeched to a halt
beside him. The officer who was driving the car alighted.
'What's the problem?' he asked.

The man, white-faced and trembling, stammered, 'It's
down there. Let me show you.' The two men stumbled
down a steep embankment which ran below the
underpass. The problem was a corpse – or what remained
of one.

The two men scrambled back up the embankment. 'Stay
in the car,' the officer told the other man, 'while I radio for
assistance. The detectives will want to talk to you. When
did you discover the body?'

'Just now. About five minutes before you pulled over.'

Detective Robert English and Sergeant Leroy Fox were
dispatched to the scene and arrived in less than ten
minutes. They found the victim to be a white male in his
mid to late twenties. He was clad in a blue check work
shirt, blue jeans and cowboy-style boots, and from the
appearance of the remains it was estimated that he had
been dead for about two days. The body was heavily

bloodstained, and the presence of blood leading down the embankment seemed to point to the victim having been thrown from the top of the bridge and having struck the slope in several places before finally rolling down to the bottom. The officers noted facial wounds which did not seem to be consistent with abrasions caused by such a fall.

The medical examiner who conducted the autopsy was able to add considerably more detail to police knowledge of the fate of the victim. When the blood-drenched clothing was removed, he was found to have been emasculated. His body had also been stabbed some twenty times with a sharp, long-bladed butcher's knife – one with a blade from seven to twelve inches long. The body had also been sliced in various places with a similar knife.

The facial wounds, which took the form of slicing on each cheek, were stated by the medical examiner to have been made with the same knife, or at least one of the same type, and he stated that the genitals had also been cut off cleanly with such a knife. They were missing and were never found.

No identification was found in the clothing beyond a matchbook found in the shirt pocket. It had originated from a Wichita Falls bar. It was unused, so the dead man might conceivably have been a non-smoker and kept it merely as a souvenir. A moderate amount of alcohol was present in the blood, but not enough to render him intoxicated at the time of death.

One of the detectives investigating the case went to the bar in Wichita Falls and showed the bartenders a photograph of the dead man reconstructed by police photographers after the autopsy. The facial wounds had been skilfully painted out and the portrait was quite lifelike. It was a good likeness, too, for it was immediately identified by several bar staff and also regulars who knew him. 'That's Billy Joe Price,' they told him. 'He was looking for work on the oil rigs. He came in last night. Sat talking with one of our regulars, Ken – I don't know his last name. Ken told the guy he worked on the oil rings and could probably find him a job. Said he would talk to someone and they'd work on it.'

Asked whether Billy Joe Price had left the bar with Ken, no one was sure, but they thought it very probable.

The next task of the police investigators was to trace Ken, but he proved elusive. He never returned to the bar, nor could he be located at any of the nearby oilfield installations. His description, together with a sketch, was prepared and passed to all patrolmen as they reported for their shifts. Copies were also sent to the police forces of neighbouring counties, together with details of the gruesome murder. The fingerprints of the dead man were checked with the FBI computer records in Washington, DC. They matched those of Billy Joe Price, a native of Norman, Oklahoma, whose fingerprints were on file on account of his having done time for burglary.

An unexpected lead developed several weeks later when deputies in neighbouring Clay County arrested one Kenneth Stogsdill, a 34-year-old unemployed former oilrigger, on a charge of attempted murder. According to the accused, he had met a motorist in a bar in Henrietta, a small town on the county border, and went with him to the caravan site where the man, a visitor to the town, was staying. According to Stogdsdill, the motorist tried to rob him and he had simply been defending himself. Occupants of adjacent caravans had heard an argument break out and shouts and screams, and called police, who found the motorist almost beaten to death with a car tyre lever. Stogsdill was arrested.

The motorist told the police a very different story from the hospital bed where he lay swaddled in bandages like a mummy, having sustained broken bones in three limbs as well as broken ribs, multiple bruises and contusions. He told investigators that he had got in conversation with Stogdsdill in a bar in the town and invited him to his caravan purely for coffee to sober up after their drinking session, but Stogsdill had made homosexual advances to him. The motorist, who was not gay, vigorously resisted his companion when he flew into a rage and attacked him. He told him forcefully that he was not gay and told him to get lost. Stogdsill then grabbed a tyre lever and launched into a frenzied attack. 'He just went plumb crazy,' the motorist said.

While Stogsdill was in jail a prison officer noted that he bore a striking resemblance to the poster which had been circulated with the sketched likeness and description of the man wanted on suspicion of murdering Billy Joe Price in the Wichita Falls area. Stogsdill maintained that he knew nothing whatever about the murder, but when samples of his hair were taken, they were found to be an exact match to hairs taken from Price's body.

In 1976 Stogsdill came to trial for the murder. He was found guilty and sentenced to die by lethal injection in the Texas Department of Corrections in Huntsville. He was also found guilty of the assault on the motorist and given a ten-year sentence. Stogsdill appealed against his conviction for murder, and the Texas Court of Criminal Appeal reversed the lower court's decision on the grounds that various legal technicalities had been infringed. Stogsdill was therefore sent for retrial to the Wichita Falls court. The court, however, had exhausted all their funds allotted to handle appeal cases and chose not to give Stogsdill a retrial. The murder conviction was dropped, and the accused was sent to prison only for the assault charge. He served only four years of his ten-year sentence before being paroled for good behaviour in 1980.

Stogsdill might well have considered himself a very lucky man to have escaped a capital murder charge so lightly, but it did not, apparently, deter him from further similar types of crime and he no doubt became over-confident and let the success of his appeal go to his head. Barely a year later he was running true to form once more.

On 2 October 1981 police were summoned to a community hospital in Denton, Texas, where a man had been admitted with a gunshot wound. He was suffering from shock as a result, but the wound, in his shoulder, was not life-threatening. The victim told the investigating officers that he was hitch-hiking home from work when a man stopped and offered him a lift. They had gone only a short distance when the driver pulled a gun and told him to drop his jeans. The hitch-hiker opened the door and jumped out of the moving car. The car was not going very fast and the hitch-hiker did not sustain any injuries beyond a few abrasions, but before he could make good his escape the driver of the car shot him in the shoulder. The car roared off at speed, but the victim managed to memorize the number of the car. A passer-by called an ambulance.

The police traced the car through the licence registration bureau to Kenneth Stogsdill, and hot-footed it to his apartment. The car was not there, and the door was locked. Stogsdill had beaten a very hasty retreat indeed, for when police forced an entry into his apartment only the landlord's fixtures remained – the fugitive had removed all his personal possessions. A surveillance was set up to watch the building in case he returned, but he was never seen there again, and his whereabouts now could be anybody's guess.

A BOLO (be on the lookout) was issued to all patrol cars and a description issued of Stogsdill and his car. A warrant was issued for his arrest, but he managed to keep the law at arm's length for more than two years. Detectives working on the case eventually had to wind down the scale of their investigations owing to the pressure of other work, but the particulars remained entered into the federal crime records, and it was these computerized records that finally enabled the law to catch up with him.

In August 1985 Kenneth Dean Beachell, a 29-year-old native of Vancouver, Washington, decided to relocate to southern California. He rang a former girlfriend, Debra Barton, who lived in San Diego. They had still kept in touch as friends. He asked Debra if he could stay in her apartment until he found work and a place of his own, and she readily agreed. That same month he moved into her apartment and within a week he had found a job as a painter and decorator with a firm specializing in the renovation and refurbishment of run-down old properties.

His first week's work finished on 5 September, he celebrated in a bar which was only a few blocks from Debra's apartment. He did not return home that night. Neither did he return to his job. Both Debra and his new employer thought it a bit odd. The firm's supervisor did not attach too much importance to it because he knew from experience that sometimes they would hire itinerant workers who worked for a week or two and then left to go elsewhere, although he did admit to police later when questioned that Beachell had not struck him as a man of that type. Debra reported her friend missing after waiting twenty-four hours, because she was convinced that he would have been in touch with her if he had had any problems, and had told her that he liked his new job and hoped to keep it.

On the morning of 11 September some small children were playing near a stream known as Rose Creek when they spotted something floating in the water. The children did not know what it was, and went over to the mother of one of them who was standing talking to a friend a few yards away. She went to look, and shouted to her friend to keep the children there with her. She stifled the urge to scream, as she did not want to frighten the children or, worse, bring them running. She was thankful that they were too young to have realized that the object 'looking like a ball' was in reality a human head.

The witness, a Mrs Alice Lockwood, took her friend aside and told her of the discovery. She asked her friend to take the children to her own home and she would call and collect her own two later. In the meantime she would call the police, and she knew that they would want her to remain at the scene as a witness. Her friend left precipitately with Mrs Lockwood's children, loudly protesting, in tow.

Police officers sent to the scene fished the head out of the water and found it to be that of a white male who appeared to be in his late twenties. His hair was thick and worn long. From the pallid appearance of the skin, they considered that the head had been in the water for some considerable time. The lower jaw was missing, and flesh had been sliced from the cheeks.

The discovery of the human head in Rose Creek set police immediately speculating as to what had happened to the rest of the body. They did not have to wait long to find out. Although they searched the creek and found no more human remains, the area of the bay adjacent to the mouth of the creek provided the answer over the next ten days, during which time several dismembered body parts, some wrapped in plastic bin liners, were washed ashore. They cordoned off the entire area until no more parts appeared.

The county pathologist Dr Robert Bucklin was assigned the job of reassembling the various body parts into some semblance of a human form. Eventually, the profile that emerged on the stainless steel autopsy table was that of a white male, 5 ft. 9 in. to 5 ft. 10 in. in height, with a probable approximate weight of 175 pounds (twelve and a half stone). The pathologist opined that the head had been severed from the body with one stroke, probably with a very sharp, long-bladed butcher's knife. The same implement, he considered, was used to slice flesh from the cheeks, to disembowel the torso and to remove the genitals. Flesh had also been sliced from the buttocks and thighs. All the body parts had been recovered over a ten-day period from the bay, except the genitals, which were never found, and the internal organs which had been removed. This led police to believe that the parts had been dumped in the bay at one point not far from the shore, where they would all naturally be washed up on land on incoming tides over a relatively short period. Strength was lent to the theory that they had been dumped not very far from the shore because there were no signs of shark attack on any of the parts.

The detectives assigned to head the investigation were Ronald Newman and Paul Olsen, together with Sergeant Eduardo Armijo. The latter contacted Detective Robert Quigley, of the Missing Persons' Bureau, who told him that a report had been filed on 7 September by Debra Barton that her friend, Kenneth Dean Beachell, had failed to report for work or come home on 6 September. Detectives were sent to interview her at her Pacific Beach apartment. She told them that she had last seen Beachell when he left to visit a bar on the evening of 6 September, saying that he would be back in a short while, and that he failed to show up at his place of employment thereafter. The detectives borrowed a photograph of Beachell from her and went back to headquarters to compare notes with the pathologist.

The hair and bone formation shown in the photograph

matched that of the head which had been found, but this was insufficient for a positive identification. Fingerprints had been taken, but were of little use as the deceased had no criminal record and thus his fingerprints were not on file. Debra Barton supplied the police with the name and address of Beachell's dentist, who sent his dental records from Vancouver, Washington, where Beachell had lived prior to his move to San Diego. Dental work carried out exactly matched the teeth in the upper jaw of the head of the dead man, confirming his identification.

Now that the identity of the murdered man was known, the next step was to find his killer. Detective Newman was sent to the bar near Debra Barton's apartment, where Beachell had headed after work on 6 September. He showed a photograph of Beachell to bartenders and regulars. A barmaid told Newman that she remembered him sitting at the bar on the night in question with a man she knew as Ken Dee. She stated that the two men stayed together until closing time. Ken Dee, she said, was a regular patron and was known to almost all the other habitués. Asked whether Beachell had left with Dee, the barmaid said that she could not be sure, but it was quite possible. She was too busy to keep tabs on everybody, she added, but when she looked up at where Dee had been sitting for most of the evening, he had gone, and so had Beachell.

The lead was promising, so Newman pressed her for more information. She told him that Dee was quite good-looking, but she had never seen him with a female companion. She said that she thought he might be gay, because she knew that he also frequented a homosexual bar in the next block.

The barmaid was able to tell Newman that Dee came into the bar on most nights and would sit at the bar chatting to other male regulars. If he did not meet someone who took more than a casual interest in him, he would leave after an hour or so, but if he met a prospective partner he would ply him with drinks and they would leave together. She took pains to point out that the bar was definitely not a gay hangout, but there was nothing she could do to discourage Dee or anyone else from using it as a pick-up place, as it was not against the law for a man to chat to other customers and buy them drinks and leave whenever they wished. Dee, she said, was discreet and avoided any ostentatious show.

'I didn't think the friendships he made were long-term relationships, more like one-night stands,' the barmaid continued, 'because the men he struck up with never came back to the bar again.' She told Newman that Dee worked as a car mechanic at a local Texaco garage which was within walking distance of the bar.

By now the detectives were pretty certain in their own minds that Dee was an alias of Stogsdill, and they took the poster with his likeness and description to the Texaco franchise owner, who confirmed that Dee certainly bore a likeness to the sketch and description on the poster. The garage owner said that Dee was a good worker, but that he apparently had some kind of health problems, because he frequently called in sick. The last day he had called in to say he was unable to report for work was, the investigators noted, the day after Kenneth Dean Beachell had gone missing. The garage owner said that Dee had not reported in for work since.

The detectives heading the investigation obtained a search warrant for Dee's apartment, in the kitchen of which they found bloodstains in the area in front of the refrigerator. They also found a veritable armoury of butchers' knives, cleavers and saws. Moving on to the living-room, the searchers soon came upon stacks of magazines dealing in gruesome detail with cannibalism, torture, bondage and various sexual perversions.

The probers now moved out to the patio, which sported several reclining chairs and hanging baskets with colourful plants in bloom. At one end, partly concealed by large planters with ferns, there stood a three-foot rubbish bin with a plastic lid. One of the officers engaged in the search was Newman. He lifted the lid of the bin and jumped hastily backwards as a foul stench assailed his nostrils. The bin was half-full of human intestines!

Although the odour was certainly discernible enough to cause unpleasant reactions, it was certainly not strong enough to suggest that the innards were those of a man who had been dead for about twenty days. They also did not look particularly decomposed and in fact had a very fresh appearance. Were they the remains of another victim, not Kenneth Beachell?

Forensic tests determined that the viscera had in fact been refrigerated for anything up to two or three weeks and had only recently been removed to the bin outside the apartment.

Some apparent joints and slices of meat, all cooked and wrapped in cling film, which had been in the refrigerator at the time of the search, were also examined by the pathologist, who determined that they were indeed human flesh. Two of the slices corresponded in size and shape to the slices removed from the cheeks of the dead man's face, while two others were found to match flesh removed from a thigh and a buttock. A fridge dish of soup was found, on forensic examination, to contain human bone marrow and small fragments of bone in addition to the more usual assortment of carrots, onions and other components.

The horrified detectives did not waste time but arrested Stogsdill as he sat in a neighbourhood bar chatting up another prospective partner – 'a prospective meal', one officer joked. Stogsdill readily admitted to his true identity and agreed that he was using the alias Kenneth Dee. He remained mute, however, when questioned about the contents of the rubbish bin and his refrigerator, and he denied all knowledge of Kenneth Dean Beachell. He was booked into jail and charged with his murder.

Stogsdill went to trial in August 1986 before Judge Michael Greer. He was defended by the public defender who had been appointed for him by the court, Alexander Liebig. The prosecutor was Pietro Mazzucco. The courtroom was packed with morbid sensation-seekers eager to learn all the grisly details which the Press had tended to omit from some of their reports in an attempt to avoid the court being besieged, but this had had little effect. Queues formed outside the courtroom in the early hours before the opening of the trial, and many were not admitted owing to lack of sufficient seats in the public gallery. Those who were admitted were frisked by police before being allowed in, because feelings ran high against the Texas Cannibal, as the Press had dubbed him.

Defender Liebig said that on behalf of his client he did not deny that Stogsdill had killed Beachell, but he argued that there was no proof of premeditation. Thus, he contended, his client was guilty only of second-degree murder. He went on to say that after Stogsdill had invited Beachell back to his apartment, an argument had developed and Stogsdill just 'blew his top' and killed Beachell on the spur of the moment. He then realized what he had done and that he would have to dispose of the body, so he dismembered it and dumped it not far from where it was found. He denied that body parts had been kept refrigerated over a three-week period, as the prosecution alleged, and some parts cooked and consumed.

Prosecutor Mazzucco strenuously refuted Liebig's contention. He said that Stogsdill was a violent man, a homosexual who was compulsively driven by fantasies of cannibalism, torture, homosexual rape, bondage and other perversions as depicted in the hard-core pornographic magazines he read. He pointed out that all the evidence proved that Stogsdill had murdered Beachell in his own home, dismembered his body, dumped some parts in the Rose Creek area of San Diego Bay, kept the intestines in his refrigerator for three weeks before putting them in the dustbin outside, and prepared some of the flesh of his victim for consumption. Since all the parts which had, according to forensic evidence, been sliced from the body were not recovered, it was to be assumed that Stogsdill had indeed consumed them prior to his arrest. This was substantiated by the fact that parts had been found in his refrigerator ready cooked and wrapped for use later. All this, Mazzucco stated, was clear evidence of premeditation.

Showing a piece of adhesive tape to which hairs and bloodstained strands from a rope still adhered, Mazzucco averred that this tape had been used to cover the victim's mouth to stop him from making any sound while he was being tortured, hanged by a rope or strangled by a noose made of rope, and having slices cut off his cheeks while he was still alive. 'The tape was used to keep the victim quiet during his last agonies,' said the prosecutor. 'Afterwards he dismembered and disembowelled his victim, keeping his internal organs in his refrigerator for three weeks before putting them in the garbage bin. He then proceeded to eat various body parts of his victim.' The jurors looked on aghast as Mazzucco outlined the grim catalogue of torture and slow death, dismemberment and cannibalism.

A surprise witness was put on the stand by the prosecution in the shape of a 32-year-old man from Vernon, Texas, who testified that he had been kidnapped at gunpoint by Stogsdill in 1975. He had been tortured and forced at gunpoint to participate in homosexual acts. Nervously the witness testified that he had been too afraid to come forward or go to the police while Stogsdill was still on the loose. 'I was afraid to identify him,' he said, 'because I was frightened that something might happen to me if I did.'

He related how he had been coming out of a cinema in Vernon when Stogsdill pulled over to the kerb and offered him a lift home. He had been foolish enough to accept, and instead of driving him home Stogsdill had driven off to a remote area, pulled a gun and subjected him to a vicious homosexual rape. He added that he himself was not a homosexual.

On 3 September 1986 the jurors, after two hours' deliberation, took the prosecutor's view and found Kenneth Stogsdill guilty of the first-degree murder of Kenneth Dean Beachell. He was sentenced to twenty-five years to life, plus an additional six years to run consecutively, for the assault in Vernon, Texas. Aged 45 at the time of his trial, he will be 76 before he is eligible for parole.

As he was driven away to prison, a milling crowd outside the court hurled eggs, tomatoes and pebbles at the police van. More restrained onlookers said that it was a waste of good eggs and tomatoes, but they could well understand the throwers' feelings. In earlier days, they said, Kenneth Stogsdill would have been lynched. 'Prison is too good for him,' one woman told a newspaper reporter. 'He should have had the chair.'

15

A Head Behind the Cooker

Fritz Haarmann (1924)

The old city of Hanover, in northern Germany, was much like any other. As well as its beautiful ancient buildings, churches, museums, historic monuments and other landmarks, it also had the inevitable underbelly of a city teeming with half a million inhabitants: a slum quarter – haunt of thieves, pickpockets, pimps, prostitutes of both sexes, conmen and swindlers, and other unsavoury characters who infested the warren-like alleyways and preyed on the young, the vulnerable and the unwary. This aspect was never more in evidence than in the years after World War I, when Germany was in the throes of post-war shortages, unemployment and poverty.

As always in such socio-economic conditions, the black market thrived, and citizens desperate to provide for their families were not slow to take advantage of it. Most of the racketeers were comparatively harmless individuals whose only concern was to smuggle goods that were in short supply and were not averse to breaking the law, but they would never kill to obtain the goods they wanted to sell. However, as with most things, there is almost always the exception to break the rule ...

A boy, born in Hanover on 25 October 1879, was to prove this exception. He was the sixth child of an engine-stoker, and was a sickly child right from the start, suffering from epilepsy and other maladies, although from all accounts these disadvantages receded as he grew to maturity. He was effeminate and passive in his ways, shunning sports and games, and avoiding fights with his fellows at school. His mother, who was seven years older than her husband, took the boy's part, and so they were close; but his father took the opposite view and felt strongly that as the lad became a teenager it was time to 'make a man of him' and put paid to what he considered to be his son's traits of weakness. Beatings and other humiliations failed to replicate the father's macho self-image in his son, and resulted only in the boy's hating his father. Eventually it was decided to send him to a military academy at Neue Breibach, but when he was found to suffer from epileptic fits he was discharged on medical grounds.

On his discharge he returned to his parents' home in Hanover and his father secured a job for him in a cigar factory owned by the boy's grandfather. Such a regimented type of employment, however, was not at all to his liking, and he made sure that he would be sacked by stealing from his employer, after which he roamed the streets and supported himself by petty thieving, pick-pocketing and burglary, for which he received a six-month jail sentence. On his release he committed a number of assaults on young boys, and his father tried to get him committed to an asylum, but the verdict of the doctors at that establishment was that the young Fritz Haarmann was not mad, just bad.

Fritz supported himself on the proceeds of crime until he was next arrested in 1903, his offences running the usual gamut of theft, breaking and entering, burglary, robbery with violence and sexual assaults on boys. After serving a total of seven years, he returned to his usual lifestyle until his next arrest in 1913 when he received five years' imprisonment for a similar series of offences.

On his release in 1918, Fritz Haarmann found post-war Germany to be a very different place from the one he had known. Law and order had broken down and chaos reigned – an ideal environment for an aspiring smuggler and master criminal. He set himself up in a basement apartment at 27 Kellerstrasse, in Hanover, and joined an organized smuggling ring, which soon made him financially secure. He then had the notion of becoming a police informer – what is known in the vernacular as a 'snout' or a 'copper's nark' – which would ensure that the police would not inquire too closely into his smuggling activities. The police liked him; Fritz was always laughing and joking with them, and it seems this bonhomie had the desired effect as a ploy to enable him to carry on his nefarious activities under their very noses without let or hindrance. He became so much 'one of them' that he soon acquired the nickname of 'The Detective'.

Emboldened by his popularity with the police, Fritz decided to branch out into a more regular source of income than smuggling. He set up business as a meat purveyor and at the same time a hawker of second-hand clothing. In the impoverished post-war Hanover meat was at a premium, and clothing likewise. People would buy on the black market without paying much heed to what the product consisted of: horsemeat, dog flesh, offal of various kinds from indeterminate animal species. As to clothing, when it was below zero outside and someone needed a warm coat for their child, who would query whether it had been stolen or not? While others looked upon the indifference of the police and the all-pervading post-war anarchy with misgivings, Fritz Haarmann saw it as an opportunist's paradise.

Hanover was the north German centre for post-war displaced persons, refugees and drifters. They tended to congregate in the precincts of Hanover's central railway station, which was not far from Fritz's rooms in the Kellerstrasse. He would join them, very much a 'street person' himself, who found their company congenial. He would befriend a homeless boy or an unemployed teenager, and offer him a bed for the night, instead of the wooden crate or cardboard box with the pathetic tatters of what had once been a blanket. He would offer a hot meal to a hungry refugee from war-torn outlying villages where food was limited to black bread and beans and small quantities at that. The desperate youths who poured off the trains that steamed hourly into Hanover would be told about the affable 'detective' who might be able to find them lodging or food, or both. Many of them hoped that he would be able to find them a job, but that was not what Fritz had in mind …

In September 1918 17-year-old Friedel Rothe disappeared. Unlike the runaways and refugees who alighted from the trains at Hanover's railway station, Friedel was a local resident, with parents who were concerned for him. They discovered that their son had chosen to frequent the railway station precincts and that he had made friends with some of the youths who congregated there. When he failed to return home one night – a thing he had never done before – they immediately went looking for him. After searching for several hours, they reported him missing to the police, who seemed to take little interest. 'You know,' they said, 'teenagers run off all the time. He is seventeen, after all. You know how it is here with jobs – maybe he's gone to Berlin to see if he can do better there.'

Friedel's parents were adamant that their son would not do such a thing, and if he had wanted to seek employment elsewhere he would have talked to them about it. 'Give it a bit longer,' the police said. 'Maybe he'll come home tonight.'

The distraught parents continued their own search without benefit of any help from the police. They questioned boys at the station, and learned that Friedel had last been seen with 'Detective' Haarmann in a billiard-hall nearby. 'Haarman!' they exclaimed. 'Why, that's the butcher and second-hand clothes dealer! What's he doing as a detective?' They went straight to police headquarters and demanded an interview with the chief. 'What's all this about Fritz Haarmann being a detective?' they demanded. 'We know him. He lives near us. He's our neighbourhood butcher and he also has a second-hand clothes stall on the market.'

'Yes, we know that,' the chief said. 'But he also works for us. Or didn't you know?'

'We've been told that Fritz was the last person to be seen with our son,' Frau Rothe said. 'We want you to go and see him at his home and question him. Right now.'

After a lot of demurring, the chief finally agreed to send an officer to see Haarmann, together with the boy's parents, at his home. The officer made a cursory search of his rooms, but found no evidence that Friedel had been there. Haarmann admitted that he knew Friedel and that he had played billiards with him in the pool-room, but denied any knowledge of his whereabouts. 'He told me he was looking for a job,' Haarmann said. 'Probably gone off to some other place to look for one. They do it all the time. Nothing for them here. Unemployment rate highest in the country.'

The parents and the police officer left, but Frau Rothe and her husband were far from satisfied. They determined to keep looking for their son and to keep questioning his associates to see if anyone else could throw any light on where he had gone after his game of billiards with the 'Detective'.

Little did they know, but at the very time they were in the kitchen of Fritz Haarmann's apartment, the boy's head, wrapped in newspaper, was lying behind the cooker ...

This close shave did not have the effect of making Fritz Haarmann more cautious – quite the reverse. He seemed to thrive on narrow escapes and is more than likely to have smiled inwardly at the grim deception he had played on his friends the police. At any event, although Friedel may have been the first of his youthful victims, he was not the last. Haarmann embarked on a grisly career of butchering teenage boys. He would kill them savagely like an animal – by his own admission at his later trial, he stated that a bite to the throat, severing the jugular vein, was his preferred method – probably unique in the annals of murder methods. After the victim had bled to death, the body would be dismembered. The parts he considered capable of being sold as 'meat joints' were kept for his butcher's stock to be sold to unsuspecting *hausfraus* who thought it was pork, while the inedible parts were cast into the River Leine which ran within a stone's throw of the Kellerstrasse. Prior to all this, the unfortunate youngsters were sexually assaulted, for Haarmann was a dyed-in-the-wool homosexual, with a predilection for adolescent boys.

In September 1919 Haarmann met 20-year-old Hans

Grans, the son of a Hanover librarian, who had run away from home a few years previously and was living on his wits. The two struck up a relationship which was not merely a homosexual alliance but was more far-reaching in its effects. The more intelligent of the pair, Grans was able to exert a more incisive influence on his friend, and on discovering that the older man's activities included murder and the sale of human flesh, he quickly got in on the act by luring boys to the basement apartment and taking his choice of the clothes they wore, if they were in good enough condition and the right size – Grans fancied himself as something of a dandy. The other clothes were, of course, added to the stock of second-hand garments sold on Haarmann's market stall. It has been claimed that Grans, who maintained a hold over his partner in crime, went so far as to order Haarmann to kill selected victims purely because Grans coveted some particular article of clothing they wore. Be that as it may, there is no doubt that Grans became fully implicated in the murders with Haarmann.

The two men moved to a tenement building in the Neuestrasse, situated on the banks of the Leine, where they rented an apartment on the second floor. This was larger than the previous place and afforded more space for the perpetration of their activities, as well as being conveniently situated for the disposal of unwanted remains under cover of darkness.

Time, however, was slowly but surely running out for Haarmann and his accomplice. Boys were disappearing in Hanover at such an unusually frequent rate that it was bound to come to the notice of the authorities, and even the lackadaisical police had to do something. Often boys were last seen – as in the case of Friedel Rothe – in the company of the 'Detective', and frantic parents would press-gang the police into visiting Haarmann in his new abode. Invariably no traces of the missing youths were found, and invariably the parents went away satisfied that the 'Detective' had nothing to do with their disappearance.

One day Haarmann met one of his neighbours on the stairs. At the time he was carrying a bucket covered by a sheet of newspaper. While they were talking, the paper slipped, and the neighbour saw that the bucket was full of blood. She was well aware, however, that Haarmann was a butcher by trade and used a room in his apartment for the preparation of animal carcases for sale; obviously he would have to dispose of the blood by pouring it down the outside drain. So this did not arouse her suspicions at all. Sounds of chopping and sawing were also heard coming from the apartment and were similarly ascribed to the processes of the butchery trade. People in the neighbourhood read almost every day in the newspapers of the disappearing boys, but nobody seemed to put two and two together ...

It did not go without notice, however, that a stream of youths entered the second-floor apartment in the Neuestrasse but were never seen to leave. This was thought rather odd, but most of the observers thought that they had gone, or been taken, there for homosexual purposes and probably left in the middle of the night so that no one would see them leaving. One astute onlooker thought that this theory was rubbish. If that were so, he said, why did they not mind being seen in broad daylight as they entered the premises? It might be worth looking into. So the observer went to the police, but got a dusty answer. They as good as accused him of being a crank with a warped sense of humour.

A woman who purchased a joint from Haarmann thought that it tasted very odd. Very odd indeed, in fact. So odd that she took it to the police and demanded that it be analysed. The police analyst pronounced it to be pork, adding that perhaps it had been kept too long and was a bit 'high'. The woman was satisfied with the explanation, but threw the remains of the joint into the dustbin.

On 11 May 1924 two boys playing on the banks of the River Leine discovered a human skull. Taken to the police, it was considered to be the work of a medical student prankster. On 24 May another skull was found, this time by a man walking his dog. The skull was considerably smaller than the first one and the police pathologist thought it to be that of a young boy of about twelve or thirteen. This time, police thought it was that of one of the missing boys who had fallen into the river and drowned. None so blind as those who will not see – or even try to.

A neighbour knocking at Haarmann's door to borrow a few clothes pegs noticed a young boy lying very still on the sofa (the front door opened straight into the living-room). She asked him who it was. Haarmann said, 'That's Gregor. Hush, don't wake him. He's asleep.' He was, indeed, asleep – for good. He was not named Gregor but Hansel Altmann, aged 15. The neighbour wondered why a young chap should be sleeping in Fritz's apartment at eleven o'clock in the morning, but thought it better not to ask too many questions.

Haarmann was taking incredible risks – part of the excitement he craved. Not only was he murdering youths at an average rate of two a week, but he was also flinging their remains wholesale into the river where they were bound to be washed up in due course. Not only was he butchering the bodies and selling their flesh for human consumption, undercutting his black-market rivals by selling the meat at rock bottom prices in order to ensure a speedy turnover, but he was even selling their clothes on his stall almost before the bodies grew cold. This was to prove his undoing.

A woman bought a pair of socks for her son on Haarmann's stall and found two large bloodstains on them. She threw them away. A man spotted Grans in the street wearing a suit which he recognized immediately as his son's best Sunday suit. His son had gone missing only two days previously. The missing boy was Hansel Altmann, the youth Haarmann's neighbour had seen 'asleep' on Haarmann's sofa when she went to borrow some clothes pegs.

Nemesis was fast catching up with the grisly pair. Newspapers all over Germany were reporting that large numbers of youths from various towns and villages who had headed for Hanover were never seen again. Suspicions which many people had prudently preferred to keep to themselves were surfacing as they read the reports. When a doctor pointed out that the second skull found on the river bank was unlikely to have become separated from the body of a drowning victim in so short a time, the police blithely came up with the far-fetched suggestion that it could have been swept downstream from a cemetery at Altfeld, where victims of a typhus epidemic had been hastily buried in mass graves. But the newspaper-reading public were not satisfied with these crude attempts to divert suspicion. So many youths disappearing, often only a few days apart and all in Hanover, could not be just a coincidence. Forced by mounting public pressure, the police chief decided to take some action. He was convinced in his own mind that the friendly, affable Fritz could not possibly be responsible, but since so many people had come forward with stories in which their chief informer was implicated, he asked two detectives investigators from the Berlin police force to come to Hanover and covertly watch Haarmann.

On 22 June 1924 the Berlin detectives spotted Haarmann at the railway station approaching a 14-year-old boy named Franz-Josef Fromm. Haarmann made homosexual advances towards him and started to touch the boy, who vigorously protested and lashed out at his attacker. A fight ensued, and the Berlin detectives separated them and arrested Haarmann for indecency. While he was in custody, it was decided to make a search of his apartment in the Neuestrasse. A squad of four police officers was sent there and were confronted with as much incriminating evidence as they would ever need. The walls were blood-splattered, as was the floor and furnishings; there was a pile of clothing and personal possessions spread out on a table, obviously intended to be sorted for his market stall. Knives, saws and choppers were lying around in the kitchen. The son of Haarmann's landlady was found to be wearing a suit which had belonged to one of the victims. And, as if more evidence were needed, some boys found a number of bones on the river bank, which were obviously human.

At police headquarters, Haarmann broke down and made a full confession to several murders, claiming that he could not remember how many, but he was quick to accuse Grans of assisting him with the murders by luring victims to their apartment. Grans was promptly arrested, still wearing young Altmann's best Sunday suit. Grans was very small and slender, which was why he was able to fit into a suit worn by a 14-year-old who was, admittedly, big for his age.

While both the partners in crime were in custody, more human remains came to light. Recent rains had swelled the waters of the River Leine and caused it to overflow its banks, leaving assorted débris lying on the surface of an adjacent meadow when the flood receded. The flotsam included a sack filled to capacity with human bones, which was sent for forensic examination to a Berlin police pathologist. He stated that the bones came from at least twenty-seven victims.

On 24 July, the day that the sack was discovered, police employed dredgers to probe the mud of the river bed. Watched by thousands of morbid onlookers lining both sides of the river banks, the dredgers brought to the surface more than 500 assorted human bones, eleven skulls and several body parts such as hands and feet. There was also a tin box containing internal organs from at least eight individuals, weighted with bricks tied to the box with rope.

On 4 December 1924 Fritz Haarmann and Hans Grans were brought to trial at Hanover Assizes. Haarmann, accused of twenty-seven murders, expressed surprise that he was being indicted for only twenty-seven murders, claiming that the total was probably nearer forty. All the known victims were aged between 12 and 20.

The fourteen-day trial was most remarkable for the way in which the accused was allowed to interrupt the proceedings at frequent intervals. He made frequent attempts at lacing the proceedings with grim humour, which brought wry smiles to the faces of the police officers who had known him, but horror to the jurors and counsel as the full story of Haarmann's infamy was revealed. He seemed to relish describing in explicit detail his sexual exploits with his victims. All the jurors were men, but even so one fainted and had to be carried out, while another asked permission to leave the courtroom as he was going to be sick. The judge adjourned the proceedings for half an hour while the two jurors composed themselves.

It was never made clear whether Haarmann had actually sampled human flesh himself. He did not admit it if he did, nor did he deny it, but it was generally supposed that his sexual perversions did not extend to cannibalism and his interest in the dead bodies was solely to sell them as meat. The woman who had partaken of the alleged 'pork joint' which she had had analysed, was present in the public section of the courtroom, and gave a shriek of horror as his proclivities were enumerated. She was rebuked by the judge, who told her to get a grip on herself.

When the prosecutor concluded his opening address, Haarmann shouted, 'You're doing fine!' from the dock, but the judge did not rebuke him. It seemed he was allowed to have his head, because none of his outbursts drew any comment from the judge. When a witness was somewhat slow in replying to a question from counsel, Haarmann shouted encouragement: 'Come on, old boy! We haven't got all day! We're here to get the truth, so tell us all you know!' Imagine a scene like that in a modern English court – he would have got short shrift and most likely taken down to the cells for contempt!

A measure of Haarmann's callous insensitivity was evident when the mother of a youth who was one of his victims broke down in the witness-box, overcome with grief. At this point the accused asked the judge for permission to smoke a cigar. Incredibly, the judge granted permission. The mind boggles ...

One day during the protracted trial Haarmann complained that too many women were being allowed into the public gallery. 'Get them all out!' he stormed. 'This is a case for men to discuss!' His request was ignored; if anything, even more women crowded into the courtroom on subsequent days of the trial.

During a later stage, when he was shown photographs of the various boys he had killed in order to identify them and say whether he had murdered them or not, he responded angrily to the suggestion that he had killed Hermann Wolf, a rather unprepossessing youth with a squint and severe facial acne. 'What do you take me for?' he demanded. 'I would never even look twice at such an ugly fellow!' The father of the boy wept during this tirade.

Lurid reports appeared each day in the German popular Press, while those in the more sedate papers were scarcely less restrained. All the reports evinced the most profound disgust, revulsion and loathing of the accused. One hundred and thirty witnesses, mostly parents and other relatives of the murdered youths, as well as neighbours whose suspicions had been aroused, including some who had not come forward until now, had come and gone in the witness-box by the time the trial ended. One such report read:

> There were scenes of painful intensity as a poor father or mother would recognise some fragment or other of the clothing or belongings of their murdered son. Here it was a handkerchief, there a pair of braces, and again a coat ... that was shown to the relatives, and to Haarmann.

A shudder ran through the court as Haarmann replied to the prosecutor's question: 'How did you kill your victims?' He persisted to the end that he had bitten them through the throat to sever the jugular vein. When told that this must have been quite a difficult thing to do, 'Not for me it wasn't,' Haarmann replied.

'But what if a boy were struggling and kicking?' the prosecutor went on relentlessly. 'Oh, that was no problem,' was the reply. 'I'd hit them over the head first to shut them up.'

'How many did you kill?' was the next question.

'Oh, I really can't remember,' Haarmann replied. 'It might've been thirty, or I think nearer forty. I can't imagine why you've charged me with only twenty-seven. That's ridiculous!'

Haarmann next launched into an account of how Grans had incited him to kill, and brought youths to the apartment for this purpose. Yet, Haarmann said, Grans was squeamish enough to prefer not to be present at the killings, and would go out for the night at these times, returning early in the morning to collect the clothes and other items he wanted. Haarmann described one occasion when Grans had come back sooner than he had expected. Hastily he shoved the corpse under the bed, but too late for Grans to avoid seeing it. Grans sat on the bed and buried his head in his hands. Haarmann sat beside him and tried to calm his accomplice. 'Don't let a little thing like a corpse upset you!' he said. The cold-blooded cynicism of this man was beyond belief.

The younger man denied every accusation Haarmann had levelled against him and strenuously denied the charges for which he was on trial, but his eventual conviction was never in any doubt. In the event, he was sentenced to twelve years in prison for his part as an accomplice.

On 19 December 1924 Fritz Haarmann was sentenced to death. The jury's unanimous verdict had been reached after only twelve minutes. Haarmann's chief concern appeared to be that he should not be found insane and sent to an asylum. Two court-appointed psychiatrists had examined him prior to sentencing and pronounced him to be legally sane.

On the last day of the trial when sentencing was to be carried out, threats were received that Haarmann would be shot in revenge by a group of the parents of murdered youths. Taking no chances, twelve armed guards were posted in front of the public gallery in the court, and another squad of armed police kept watch outside the courtroom. The court was packed to capacity, and at least seven or eight hundred people milled outside for whom there had been no room in court. After he had been sentenced to death, Haarmann stated that he was not intending to appeal. The Butcher of Hanover asked no mercy. 'Justice will be served,' he said, 'if they behead me.'

He got his wish. The following day he was executed by decapitation in the prison yard in Hanover, on 20 December 1924. He had spent his last night in prison smoking his favourite cigars, eating a frugal meal of bread and cheese and coffee, and playing draughts with his guards.

The mothers and fathers of teenage boys in Hanover could now breathe easily once more. The foulest mass murderer in Hanover's history had at last been run to earth.

The *hausfraus* who had patronized Haarmann's butchery

business no longer asked the police to have their joints, chops or steaks analysed. But it is more than just a rumour that after the trial a good many of them became vegetarians.